Drawing and Perceiving

Real-World Drawing for Students of Architecture and Design

Fourth Edition

Douglas Cooper

BICENTENNIAL

1807
WILEY
2007

BICENTENNIAL

John Wiley & Sons, Inc.

For general information about our other products and services, please contact our Customer Care Department within the United States at (800) 762-2974, outside the United States at (317) 572-3993 or fax (317) 572-4002.

Wiley also publishes its books in a variety of electronic formats. Some content that appears in print may not be available in electronic books. For more information about Wiley products, visit our web site at www.wiley.com.

Library of Congress Cataloging-in-Publication Data:

Cooper, Douglas, 1946–
    Drawing and perceiving : life drawing for students of architecture and design / by Doug Cooper. —4th ed.
        p. cm.
    Includes bibliographical references and index.
    ISBN-13: 978-0470-04716-3 (paper/cd)
    ISBN-10: 0-470-04716-X (paper/cd)
    1. Architectural drawing—Technique. 2. Visual perception. I. Title.
    NA2708.C66 2007
    720.28'4—dc22

Printed in the United States of America

10 9 8 7 6 5 4 3 2 1

Contents

Preface

Several years ago I heard a story from an alumnus of Carnegie Mellon University about Henry Hornbostel, the great Beaux Arts architect and designer of the original Carnegie Tech campus. Hornbostel had also served as the first Dean of the College of Fine Arts.

It seems he had been brought into a design competition for a major public commission at the end of the process because the jury was dissatisfied with the entrants' submissions. The jurors were hoping they might get some inspiring ideas from Hornbostel, and so they invited him to inspect the site from an overlooking hill. Hornbostel had huge hands. And so when they asked him what he might propose, he simply whipped out his left hand, took a pen in his right, and there on his tablet-sized hand proceeded to draw a perspective rendering of what he might do. The amazed jury nearly awarded him the commission on the spot.

The kind of drawing that is most important for students in the design fields is exactly the kind Hornbostel demonstrated on that hill long ago: drawing that is second nature, drawing that is quick, drawing that can win the commission, drawing that comes right out of the finger tips and straight from a knowledge of the real physical world. And this sort of drawing is all the more important now that, post-computer, most of the work of perspective projection and shadow casting is no longer necessary. How can we get this ability?

It doesn't happen over night. Courses that emphasize expression at the expense of observation miss the point. And it doesn't come from drawing that emphasizes appearance over three-dimensional understanding. Hornbostel could draw convincingly on that hilltop because he understood the three-dimensional implications of the marks he set down. His was not a painterly understanding. It was informed by years of building and years of drawing what he built.

Drawing ability comes from three sources. It arises in the hand—almost as an athletic issue, the hand must move well. It arises in the intellect—the structure of the world must be understood. And it arises in conception —ultimately drawing must impart order to what is drawn. In this the fourth edition, I have tried to address these three aspects: the first chapter addressing the body, the second the mind, and the third the spirit.

Acknowledgements

Teaching begins and ends with students. Their successes are the great pleasure of teaching. In more than 30 years of teaching, I have taught over 2,000 students, and their drawings are the heart of this book. I have also worked with many able colleagues. Professor John Pekruhn was the senior instructor of the course when I first came to Carnegie Mellon University. He along with Robert Skydell assisted during the first two years I taught and provided much needed advice. Paul Ostergaard, Raymond "Bud" Mall (some of whose photographs appear in this volume), Andrew Tesoro, and John Ritzu were important in the implementation of the exercises in the book's first and second chapters. Thereafter Janice Hart, Jim Quinnan, and Barry Shields have taught freehand drawing and watercolor, and Dana Buntrock, Mark English, Bruce Lindsey, Laura Lee, Laura Nettleton, Paul Rosenblatt, and Nino Saggio have taught freehand drawing and perspective. Rebecca Schultz has provided illustrations that have appeared in recent editions. Daryl Gleiche has produced the ink drawings showing shadow projection in perspective. I am grateful to my wife Meg and two daughters, Laura and Sarah, for their helpful support for and comments about my teaching. It has been a huge treat in this edition to also include images from my daughter, Sarah, who is now a photographer living in Sweden. I also have used images from several murals I've done to illustrate points in the text. Patty Clark, Jonathan Kline, Grégoire Picher, Rebecca Schultz, John Trivelli, and both daughters, Laura and Sarah, have all played roles in these. I want to thank the TAs in my course. Without their loyal support, it would be impossible to teach the course I teach. I am indebted to Brian Parker and Carnegie Mellon's Network Media Group for the superb job they did in filming and producing the videos for the CD that accompanies this book. As I've brought this edition to a close, my partner, Stefani Danes, has provided many helpful comments both about the videos and the book's overall structure. Of all people, this book owes its greatest debt to Professor Kent Bloomer of Yale University. The assignments, criticism, and encouragement of that great educator originally led to my interest in drawing.

I.1 Opposite: Quelcy Kogel.

Introduction

I.2 Right: Early in his career Louis Kahn took extensive sketching tours to the Mediterranean. Louis Isidore Kahn, (American, 1901–74) *Towers, San Gimignano,* 1929. Watercolor and red pencil on paper. Williams College Museum of Art. Museum purchase with funds provided by an anonymous donor and with the J.W. Field Fund, John B. Turner '24 Memorial Fund, Joseph O. Eaton fund, Karl E. Weston Memorial Fund, Bentley W. Warren Fund 94-14. San Gimignano, (ca. 1928).

I.3 Far right: It seems unmistakable that the bold and simple sense of mass that characterized his later work was first practiced in those sketches. Louis I. Kahn, Alfred Newton Richards Medical Research Building, University of Pennsylvania, Philadelphia, PA, (1957–61), Louis I. Kahn Collection, University of Pennsylvania and the Pennsylvania Historical and Museum Commission.

I.4 When his practice takes him to distant cities, Ray fills his sketchbook with drawings of urban spaces. Ray Gindroz, Urban Design Associates.

DRAWING AND PERCEPTUAL THEORY

Early in his career, architect Louis Kahn took extensive sketching trips to the Mediterranean region. Today, with the knowledge of his subsequent career in mind, it seems unmistakable that the bold and simple sense of mass and volume that so characterized his later work was first practiced there in the simple pastel and wash studies of towns and rock formations he made while traveling.[1]

When his practice takes him to new cities, Pittsburgh urban designer Ray Gindroz brings along a sketchbook, which he fills with contour drawings of urban spaces. Though Ray does not intend to rebuild St. Petersburg of the Romanovs or *fin-de-siècle* Paris (cities he recently visited) in today's world, these sketches play an important though indirect role in his practice. His annotations indicate as much. They state how the architecture in each scene articulates such concepts as levels of privacy, way finding, and grandeur: important concerns for an urban designer of any age. With his sketches Ray seems to be creating a self-renewable primer on the ways and means of urban design.

[1] *The Travel Sketches of Louis I. Kahn* (Pennsylvania Academy of the Fine Arts, Philadelphia, 1978).

The young German architect Thomas Spiegelhalter acknowledges a course he took in classical anatomy with its emphasis on the unified structure of the skeleton and muscle groups as one of the key experiences in the way he now thinks about the structure of buildings. Le Corbusier based his modular system on the measure of the human body.

Using the natural and man-made world as a source for the inspiration and order of design is nothing new. The sketchbooks of Leonardo Da Vinci alternate so seamlessly back and forth between drawings of real objects and proposals for visionary constructions that the conclusion that one was exercise for the other is inescapable. Much in the spirit of the above-mentioned Louis Kahn, 18th-century British delineator Thomas Gandy drew upon his sketches of rock formations in the landscape to create the atmospheric renderings that so inspired the work of his employer, the architect Sir John Soan.

This book prepares students to draw the real world. Its relationship to actual practice is implicit but indirect. This book is not about drawing media, though several are practiced, and students will gain considerable skill in them through the book's exercises. This is not a book about what is called "design drawing," though I assume young designers will also (as they should) use its techniques in their design process. Underlying this book is an assumption: that through closer observation and understanding of the real physical world, designers come to a deeper understanding of the elements of design.

Each of the book's three chapters presents real-world drawing with a specific theory of perception in mind, and each chapter's exercises presume (and illustrate with student drawings) the understanding of vision specific to each theory. Against this clear background, work can be more focused and criticism more objective.

Chapter 1: Engaging the Visual World

The first chapter is built on the *transactionalist*[2] understanding of perception and adapts the exercises of Kimon Nicholaides from his superb text, *The Natural Way To Draw.*[3] It focuses on interaction with the environment as the key issue of drawing. It asserts that drawing is an active, kinesthetic and tactile process. The hand moves. Marks are made. The focus is more on the act itself—making marks and interacting with what is drawn—and less on what the viewer brings to the process or the nature of what is drawn.

Nicholaides' understanding is absolutely appropriate to the task that designers

I.5 The first chapter asserts that drawing is an active, kinesthetic and tactile process. Yoonsun Yang.

---

[2] A view of perception that emphasizes the role of interaction with the environment as a basis for perception. Leading proponents of this point of view are Adelbert Ames and John Dewey.
[3] Kimon Nicholaides, *The Natural Way to Draw* (Boston: Hougton Mifflin, 1941).

I.6 The second chapter is aimed at building knowledge of the visual world as it exists and drawing as a reasoned response to that order. Ju-Kay Kwek.

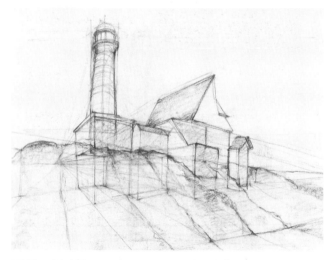

I.7 The third chapter is more proactive. It frames drawing as a process of projecting order out into the visual world. Xianghua Wu.

ultimately face. They must create objects that do not yet exist: they make things. Appropriate to this task, Nicholaides conceived of drawings as physical analogues of what is represented. To go a step further, he considered drawing itself to be an act of *making.* He believed drawings should not be mere imitations, but real in themselves.

Chapter 2: The Appearance of the Visual World

The second chapter focuses on the nature of what is being drawn: the three-dimensional world. It is based on the early work of perceptual psychologist, James J. Gibson, originator of the so-called *ecological* view of perception. Because it is central to his understanding that sensation is already ordered in itself, Gibson's work is particularly useful for architects and designers who, as a matter of course, must assume the prospect of a general order. The exercises of Chapter 2 have an analytical character. They are aimed at building knowledge of the order of the visual world as it exists and drawing as a reasoned response to that order. The second chapter's extensive coverage of perspective is built on his understanding of the relationship of geometry to appearance.

Chapter 3: When Order is Made

Based loosely on Gestalt psychology, the third chapter considers what the artist brings to the process. Order originates with the persons making drawings and the conceptions they apply to the process. Drawing becomes a process of projecting order out into the world. Perspective, light, and color, are all addressed from this proactive stance.

Videos

I have prepared a set of videos that illustrate the process of many of the exercises in each chapter. These provide important insights into the ways in which these various approaches actually impact drawing.[4]

How students learn

Along the way, it is important to recognize how students learn and how they don't. They don't learn in a linear way: each day a little better than the day before. Rather they learn (and show progress) more in fits and starts: with sudden leaps forward—sometimes from one drawing to the next—after long periods in which little progress is evident. I suspect the reason has to do with information and skill processing.

Years ago I lived in Germany, and I learned to speak German reasonably well the old fashioned way: by living there. I remember progress seemed to come in a curious way. One day I would make a connection—say that clauses preceded by *daß* ("that" in

---

[4] Video services provided by The Network Media Group, Carnegie Mellon University. Videography by: Brian Parker, David Dyke, Dave Joubert. Editing by Brian Parker.

German) always have their verbs at the end. The next day I would incorporate this new knowledge into my speech. But then curiously on a subsequent day I often felt I was slipping backwards. It all seemed puzzling until one day I realized that each forward step was also making me aware of all those things I had been able to ignore (necessarily so) until that advance. Each forward step, in effect, only opened up a Pandora's box of new issues to address—something that seemed puzzling at first because of the apparent sense of confusion it left in its wake.

This fact of learning is something every student and teacher (of any subject) needs to accept. Shown below are drawings from Carolyn Caranante over several classes during a two-week period in fall 2005. For a while (drawings 1, 2) her work seemed to just bump along, never showing much progress, sometimes even seeming to get worse. But then during the second week (drawings 3, 4), she suddenly understood the unified structure underlying perspective (drawing the car was key), and her drawing then remained at that improved level. If I could diagram it, progress is never like the graph at top right, usually more like the middle one, and at times—my experience in learning German—more like the bottom graph.

In Toto

With the three distinct approaches to perception and drawing outlined above, a student gains a complete picture of how to draw the man-made and natural world. Whatever the subject or intention, one ultimately proceeds with various proportions of these three approaches in the mix—the first chapter having been directed at the body, the second at the mind, and the third at the spirit. In that it addresses all three, it is my hope that *Drawing and Perceiving* may serve as that one book on the subject of real-world drawing for architects and designers if one would have only one book to buy.

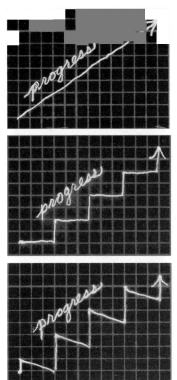

I.8 Alternative diagrams of progress.

I.9 Progress in the work of Carolyn Caranante over a two-week period.

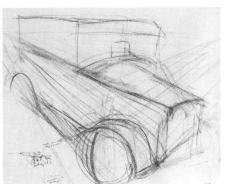  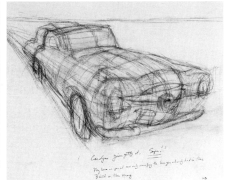 

Engaging the Visual World

TOUCHING AND MOVING
PROVIDE THE FOUNDATION

Suspicions about vision

A bird in the hand is worth two in the bush is an adage of hunting. Though it points to the uncertainties of marksmanship, it also hints at the limitations of vision when not affirmed by the sense of touch. Likewise, when in some blissful moment, we are wont to say, "Touch me, prove I'm not still dreaming," we do so in recognition that it is through the sense of touch that we come closest to verifying the realness of things and events. Suspicions about vision originate in the fact that, despite its obvious usefulness, vision is less essential than the sense of touch. Imagine a world without sight, and we are impressed by the prospect of the difficulty of daily life. Imagine a world without touch, and we must wonder if life would be demonstrable or even possible.

What is so useful about vision is that it provides information at a distance. After some life's experience, the unfolding image of an approaching car offers sufficient warning in itself; warning that is sufficient without the confirming crunch that would result from remaining in the middle of the road. Vision allows for a certain useful detachment from life, at more than arm's length and out of harm's way. But it is precisely for this capacity that we must consider vision a kind of surrogate sense, one step removed from the "nitty-gritty" of real life.

The fact that vision alone provides a somewhat detached sense of reality was particularly evident in the televised reporting of the recent wars in the Persian Gulf. I refer here to those chilling (and riveting) videos tracking smart bombs to their targets. So

1.0 Overleaf: Engaging the Visual World. Douglas Cooper with Patricia Clark and Grégoire Picher. Lake Union (collage detail) from the mural series: *From these Hills, from these Valleys,* King County Courthouse, Seattle, WA, 2005. Charcoal and acrylic on paper on board. 14' x 12'.
1.1 Opposite: Touching and movement provide the foundation. Douglas Cooper with Patricia Clark and Grégoire Picher. Mining and Logging, from the mural series: *From these Hills, from these Valleys,* King County Courthouse, Seattle, WA, 2005. Charcoal and acrylic on paper on board. 9' x 12'.

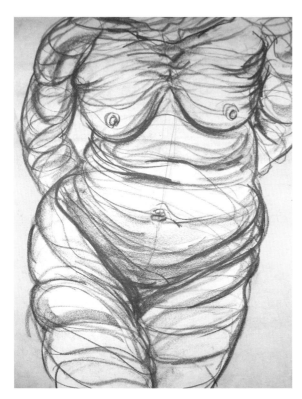

1.2 When students draw contours, they begin by imagining their pencil is actually touching that surface. Unknown artist.

complete was our detachment that, as we watched, we also lost any sense of the human beings there at the target and the pain and suffering inflicted upon them. The all-too-droll voice-over commentary of the newscasters said as much. From the comfort of the living room, our perception remained confined to the visible, out of touch, and free of pain.

If only because it is so easily deceived, there is ample cause to distrust the primacy of vision. Camouflage in warfare, *trompe l'oeil* in painting, and cinematic special effects are all examples of the relative ease with which the eye can be fooled.

Some perceptual psychologists, in particular the *transactionalists,* believe that touch and movement play key supportive roles for vision. They believe all perception, most particularly vision, is learned through a process of interaction (transaction) with the environment.[1] In their view, a baby learns to see by verifying the visual field through much kicking, grasping, and crawling about; a hitter in baseball learns to see and hit a curve ball by much swinging (and missing); and a drawing student learns to see the world in perspective by first making lines converge to common vanishing points.

Vision insufficient for drawing

If vision by itself is insufficient for the perceptions of daily life, is it equally suspect as a foundation for learning to draw? My own doubts about its role originated years ago in a review I was conducting of my teaching. By chance, at the time of my review, I was reading a book about drawing, *The Natural Way to Draw* by Kimon Nicholaides.[2] Reading his book gave me a sudden insight into some of my students' problems. Earlier, I had observed that the drawings of those who had subsequent difficulty in design drawing had lacked a quality evident in the work of those who had not. Where their drawings seemed inactive and purely visual, those of their more successful colleagues, though often less skillful, seemed gestural, rough, and tactile by comparison. It occurred to me that a focus on the purely visual aspects of drawing at the expense of a kinesthetic and tactile foundation might lead to a later inability to use drawing effectively as a design tool.

Much of what Nicholaides wrote in introducing his exercises seemed to indicate a distrust of vision. I even got the impression he considered vision unaided by the sense of touch to be almost voyeuristic in its detachment.

Suitability for architects and designers

Nicholaides' exercises require intense physical involvement with subjects from the outset. Usually he frames the act of drawing in a way analogous to touching. When students draw contours, they begin by imagining their pencil is actually touching the surface of the figure. When they model surfaces, they begin by imagining that the charcoal is actually manipulating that surface.

For its relationship to design, the modeling exercise is particularly interesting (see page 45). Before modeling its surface, Nicholaides asks students to build a figure's mass. To do this, they have to think of the charcoal as equivalent to a real material. They start at the figure's core and build out, mark upon mark about that core, until they reach the outer surface. Then after having, in effect, already built the figure, they model its surface. In the end these drawings acquire a heavy character that does not necessarily match the appearance of these people at all. But they are *made* like them, and this attribute points to the reason why Nicholaides' exercises are so well suited to the task that architects and designers face.

Architects and designers must design something that does not yet exist. Whereas the work of a painter might legitimately remain focused on the reception and interpretation of sensation from the visual world,[3] that of the architect and designer must be directed squarely at the task of constructing something that does not yet exist.

Consistent with this aim, the modeling exercise (and, to a less obvious degree, the others as well) presents the act of drawing as an act of making a thing rather than just viewing that thing. And as Nicholaides sets it up, making precedes viewing. Before we can model a figure, we have to first make it exist on the page. For the architect or designer faced with the task of designing something that does not yet exist, no other approach makes sense. If trained to draw only that which is already visible, how could they begin to draw when nothing is yet there to draw? What first marks could they make?

Ever since, I have used Nicholaides' exercises in my course. I have found it works well to introduce them, as Nicholaides did: using the figure. Figure drawing sessions have a matchless intensity and focus that makes for a good beginning. Then we apply each exercise to architectural subjects. Like the figure drawing exercises preceding them, these exercises build architectural drawing on Nicholaides' firm foundation. When we draw, we do not just imitate an object's appearance. On the page before us, we consider each drawing to be real in itself. That is Nicholaides' great gift.

1.3 When students model surfaces, they begin by imagining that their charcoal is actually manipulating that surface: pushing some areas back and allowing other areas to come forward. Unknown artist.

---

[1] Principal advocates of this position are Adelbert Ames and John Dewey.

[2] Kimon Nicholaides, *The Natural Way to Draw* (Boston: Hougton Mifflin, 1941).

[3] Impressionism would be an example.

NICHOLAIDES AND CONTOUR

Movement is the basis of contour

Nicholaides' interest in contour as a fundamental issue for drawing grew out of his work with the Camouflage Corps in France during World War I. As part of his job, he had to study and work extensively with contour maps. The level contours these maps represented are not, of course, just a convention of map-making. Contours are rooted in the patterns of mankind's inhabitation of the land throughout history: whether tea terraces in Sri Lanka or rows of grapevines in the hills of Tuscany. Thus as Nicholaides' use of contour maps progressed, he grew fascinated with the rich and readable sense of the landscape they conveyed. Later he incorporated the issue into his teaching at the Art Students' League in New York. In the end, contour became so central to his conception of drawing that it became the topic that opens his book, *The Natural Way to Draw*. What is so compelling about contour?

One of the most powerful images in my childhood was an illustration I found in a book about the life of Roland, the legendary knight of King Charlemagne's 9th-century France. The painting showed Charlemagne's army being led over the Alps by a magical elk with glowing horns. However, what so fascinated me about this scene was not the elk, but the way in which the long line of foot soldiers and mounted knights snaking up over the pass so powerfully portrayed the landscape itself. It was as if their movement on the land also revealed the land.

In my mind ever since, the subject of contour has been linked with the experience of moving across the landscape. Much as for the drivers on the interstate at left, pathways and the prospect of moving on their contours "over hill and dale" have seemed to make

1.5 It was as if their movement on the land also revealed the land. Charlemagne Crossing the Alps. Illustration by Peter Hurd. Reprinted with the permission of Scribner, an imprint of Simon & Schuster, from *The Story of Roland* by James Baldwin. Copyright © 1930 by Charles Scribner's Sons.

1.4 Opposite: Movement is the basis of contour. Douglas Cooper with Sarah Cooper. *Pennsylvania Turnpike Mural* (western panel), Pennsylvania Turnpike Commission Headquarters, Harrisburg, PA, 2001. Charcoal and acrylic on paper on board. 7' x 13'.

1.6 The roadway's twisting contour so sharpened my friend's perception of the drop-off.

the landscape visible from afar; just *how* visible was made clear to me several summers ago by some friends of mine.

They were driving over the Furka Pass in Switzerland. It is a torturous sequence of switchbacks and steep grades. Just as they got over the crest to begin their descent and upon seeing the view before them, everyone in the car suddenly stopped talking. Snaking down the slope and shining in the sunlight, the road dropped away steeply into the valley—but with no guardrail at all! And without any rail, the twisting contour down the slope so sharpened their sense of the sheer drop-off that what had been a nice summer's drive became a white-knuckle descent.

Had I been in the car at the time, I might have tried reassuring them by saying, "it may not be as bad as it looks," and I would have said so because ultimately, *the only real basis for establishing the form of a surface is actually moving on that surface.* Much of our childhood experience of learning to see is preoccupied with just that: establishing the connection between what vision provides from afar and the reality of the actual experience. Thus we once learned to establish the visual fact of a bend in the road by first walking along it and even the flatness of a frozen pond by first skating upon it. To a certain extent even the collective understandings of our society at large are only finally established by the verification of actual movement. How many skeptics about the roundness of the Earth must have remained still in 16th-century Spain even after Columbus' voyage—remained that is until Magellan's crew finally sailed around it and returned 1519–1522. In the end, the proof is always in the moving.

Beyond shape, the qualities of surfaces are established through movement as well. A placid lake provides a smooth crossing for canoeists, and white-water rapids an experience that is quite a bit rougher. Smooth and rough are each characteristics of crossing surfaces. Our perception of even the most subtle qualities of surfaces rests ultimately on movement. Before a purchase, a woman in a clothing store will verify the fineness of a silk garment by running her fingers across it.

Knowing contours from afar

But though real physical movement does underlie our understanding, once we've learned to interpret them, visual contours eventually do provide sufficient information about surfaces without our ever having to actually touch them or cross them. In effect they come to offer the experience of movement, but from afar. This is vision's great gift.

For an observer on shore, the visual contours of canoeists on a smooth lake or on white water rapids are sufficient in themselves for understanding. In the first instance, the gentle waves and unbroken reflections of the boat and paddlers and, in the second instance, the turbulent water and canoe all akimbo are adequate to discern the distinct nature of each experience. We don't actually need to get in the canoe and paddle or get wet to know what each is like.

And so it was for my friends on the Furka Pass. They could "feel" the steepness from the visual contours of the road alone. They could feel fear from the top of the pass before they even began their descent.

1.7-8 For an observer on shore, the contours are sufficient for understanding. Line drawings based on paintings by Winslow Homer.

1.9 S. Maria dei Fiori, Florence. Photo: H. Saalman.

1.10 Side Chapels, Orvieto.

1.11 Composite columns, Siena. Photo: H. Saalman.

Knowing surface from afar

The material properties of surfaces offer a similar kind of information: the experience of movement from afar. This is particularly the case with objects that have a good deal of surface texture. Years ago I spent six months in Tuscany. In nearly every town in the province, I found striped churches with alternating courses of black and white marble. One reason for the stripes is to signify use. In Tuscany only religious buildings have stripes. Secular buildings have none. But I was also struck by the extent to which these stripes seemed to articulate form. All these churches have very readable forms. This is the case whether we are considering whole structures such as Brunelleschi's octagonal cupola in Florence, building parts such as the apsidal side chapels at Orvieto, or details such as the composite columns at Siena. The stripes make all these forms graphically apparent.

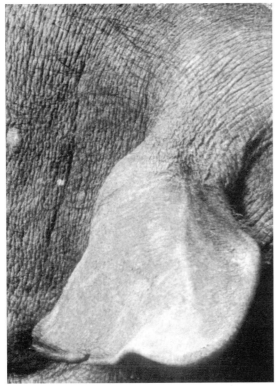

1.12 Neck of a warthog. Photo: Raymond Mall.

1.13 Basket made of reeds.

1.14 Legs with fishnet stockings. Photo: R. Mall.

The same is true of more ordinary objects as well, whether natural or artificial. We perceive the shape of the neck of the warthog in Figure 1.12 on the basis of the curving pattern of creases on its skin; similarly we perceive the roundness of the basket in Figure 1.13 on the basis of its pattern of woven reeds. Though touching these objects would surely enrich our understanding, we do not absolutely need to touch them to know that they are round. The eye learns to follow the paths the hand once traveled.

Sometimes objects lack sufficient contour or surface texture to be easily perceived. In such instances, we sometimes augment or exaggerate their material properties to make their form more apparent. This practice, evident in the striped churches of Tuscany, lies at the heart of decoration. Fishnet stockings on a Las Vegas showgirl and chrome stripes on a 1950s car are each in their own way intended to show off form by adding greater levels of contour to a surface.

1.15 1953 Buick Skylark. Photo: Sarah Cooper.

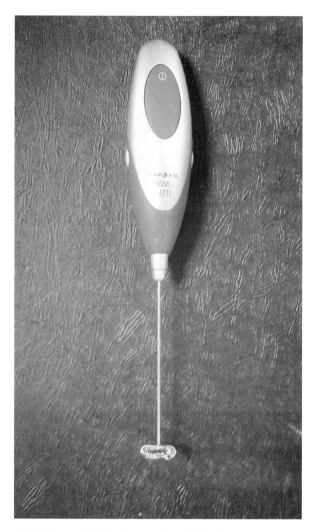

1.16 Above: Milk frother, Bonjour Primo Latte.
1.17 Above right: Cemetery, Enric Miralles, Bilbao, Spain. Photo: Bruce Lindsey.

Surface contour and design

For an architect, knowledge of material contours becomes a key issue for the design of building elevations. In the example above of Enric Miralles' cemetery in Bilbao, Spain, the pre-cast concrete shelves, which line the ascending walkway, articulate the walkway's rise by also *stepping up* that same slope themselves.

For the designer of the milk-frother at left, care had to be taken to ensure the contours of the various parts of the handle would underscore the handle's hand-friendly shape. However, articulation of shape or surface form are not the only issues that arise with contour. The orientation of users of a building, even their sense of the visual stability of an environment, can be at stake.

Frank Gehry's fabulous Guggenheim Museum in Bilbao, Spain, is a good instance to cite. The environment visitors walk through is complex. The forms are not rectangular.

1.18 Above left: Guggenheim Museum, Bilbao, Spain.
Frank Gehry. Photo: Bruce Lindsey.
1.19 Above middle: Allison Lukacsy.
1.20 Above right: Be patient. As with learning a sport,
it takes time to get your hand and vision in sync.

The shapes are not familiar. And a queasy ill-at-ease could have easily been the result, had Gehry not carefully kept the horizontal contours of the metal cladding plainly evident to assure a readable sense of surface.

The contour exercises

The contour exercises that follow retrace the line of thought presented so far. In the spirit of verifying the visual field kinesthetically at the outset, they will begin with touch and movement before turning to vision alone. To deepen your sense of the primacy of physical movement as the basis for vision, be attentive to the motion of your hand and eyes as you draw. Move slowly and deliberately at the start. Later vary your speed. To build your sense of visual contours on the firm basis of real and familiar physical knowledge, we will start with the human figure before drawing other objects. Be patient! As with learning any sport, it takes time to get your hand and vision in sync.

CONTOUR 1
Follow your eyes
Felt-tipped pen, bond paper.

ON
THE
CD

Look at some point along a contour on the model and imagine your pen is actually touching the model. Let your eyes slowly move along that contour. Then in one continuous line, let your pen follow the movement of your eyes as they follow the contour across the surface of the model. Draw slowly and deliberately. Look only occasionally at the page and keep believing your pen is touching the model. Do not draw only profiles, but do seek contours moving across the form. After several drawings, include background elements, an object across the room for example, and note the apparent reduction in size.[4]

---

[4] Adapted from "Contour," in Kimon Nicholaides, *The Natural Way to Draw* pp. 9–14.

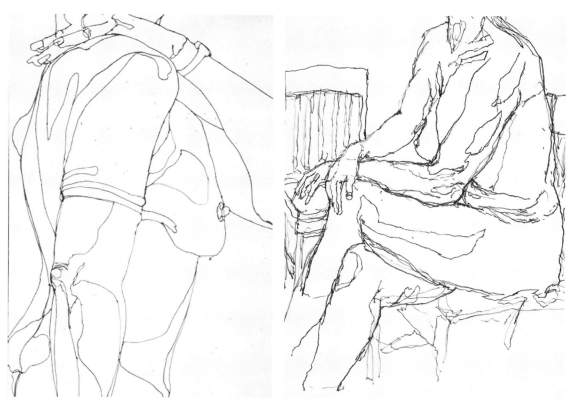

1.21 Jonathon Kline.

1.22 See on demonstration CD.

Contour and surface

How does our experience of surface relate to our experience of contour in exercises like the one above? A brief story. One summer afternoon my daughter Laura and I were on a back terrace when she observed tiny bits of shiny foil wrapper moving slowly in a zigzag course up a set of nearby steps. Looking closer we saw two thin columns of ants: one carrying foil bits to a nearby colony and the other returning for more. (Earlier we had shared a chocolate bar and had left the wrapper on a nearby brick.) The line of ants was several meters long before it vanished into a nearby flowerbed. For the next several minutes, Laura and I amused ourselves putting obstacles in their path, which the ants then had to climb over on their way back and forth. The ants had no choice. They were on the surface. Their long lines were fixed to it. So up the risers, across the treads and over our many barriers, they tirelessly carried their booty along the contour we had set for them.

Like the path the ants were following that day, contour lines in a drawing are all about surface—they remain on it. Though tireless (like the ants) in following every zig and zag, their spirit should be one of pure joy in movement. They should have the same mood as a relaxed summer drive through the countryside, with no exact destination and no appointments to keep. On such days you turn off main roads. You follow small lanes. Whimsy and spontaneity guide you. Such moods should guide your line-work.

The incremental nature of contour drawing is one of its most transformative characteristics—one in which distortion plays a natural role. Step by step it proceeds, initially with little visual governance over holistic properties of proportion and shape. Welcome this prospect. Don't expect a contour drawing to result in perfect likeness. The most important issue is the experience of moving on a surface and moving your eyes in concert with that surface. In any event, distortion lies at the heart of expression.

Cross contours, lines that move away from profiles and across the form, are sometimes difficult to find. If you have difficulty—you may have to imagine them or find them in subtle variations in skin color—have the model wear some elements of clothing to make them easier to find. The armlet the model is wearing in the drawing at far left is one such instance.

When contours make space

It is a startling experience to jump (as the drawing near left does) from the outside profile of one figure to some object or person in the background. You should note of course the apparent reduction in size between foreground and background; people in the background may seem surprisingly small by comparison to the foreground person with which you started. However, there is also a more profound transformation. The drawing suddenly becomes three-dimensional. What until that moment showed just an object in isolation, a person, suddenly becomes a view. It is a no less startling transformation than would have been the case had the ants in our backyard suddenly taken flight around the barriers we had placed in their way. While contour drawing is all about surface, ultimately with such jumps, it is also about escaping surface by perceiving edges and overlapping edges. In that escape contour drawing trancends the tactile and becomes truly visual.

1.23 The incremental nature of contour drawing is one of its most transformative characteristics. Jo Frost.

CONTOUR 2
Vary the width of the line
<u>Stick, india ink, bond paper</u>

Find a short branch about 6 inches long and a quarter inch in diameter. A slight bow in the stick is good, and you can leave the bark on. Cut off one end so the stick has a quill-like edge somewhat like a calligraphy pen. Dip your stick into the India ink and draw the contour of the model much as you did in Contour 1.

Vary the width of the line. Roll the stick in your fingers and rotate your wrist as you draw. Let the line get thick and dark along some contours that seem more expressive or important. Then let it get thin and even vanish altogether at other places.[5]

---

[5] Adapted from "Contour," in Kimon Nicholaides, *The Natural Way to Draw* pp. 9–14.

1.24 Above: Yu Hsien Chia.
1.25 Below left: Erin Nunes.

Contour and line variation

So far we have not varied lines at all. Now we'll start. Line variation must be learned by doing and at the outset by letting go of control. When you draw with crude tools like the stick and ink used above, the novelty alone makes lines difficult to control. Don't try to control them. Give your hand and arm time to master their unpredictability on their own.

Roll the tool in your fingers—a bent stick helps. Alternate exposing a corner and the stick's full breadth. A varied line automatically results: thin vs. thick. If you let them, such variations can express formal properties in your subject. In Figure 1.25, the fleeting line on the hip expresses its bulge. Thicker lines express the more recessed and shaded areas behind the arm and beneath the hip. The heavier line on the top of the knee serves to pull it forward of the breast. Gradually incorporate such properties into your work.

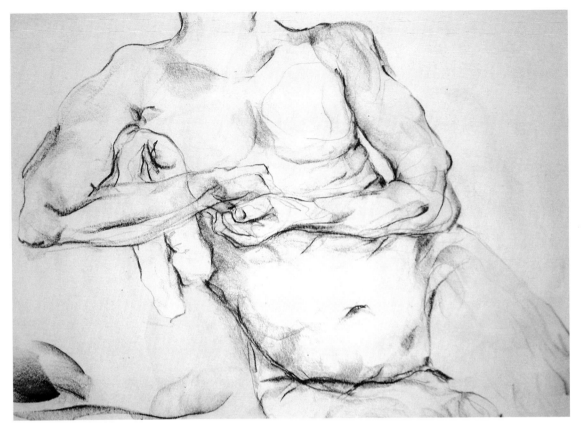

1.26 Above: unknown artist.
1.27 Below right: See on demonstration CD.

CONTOUR 3
Vary the character of the line
<u>*Conté crayon, newsprint*</u>

ON THE CD

Conté crayon allows you to vary the darkness of a line by changing the pressure of your hand. In addition, by rolling the stick in your fingers, you can change a line's width. It will be pointed if you use a corner, wider if you use a full edge, and wider still if you use an entire side. Take advantage of these possibilities to express varying levels of importance among contours. Some may carry a greater sense of the form. Others, such as overlapping edges, may record important spatial relationships. In a playful manner, always in a playful manner, give these lines greater weights.[6]

[6] Adapted from "Contour," in Kimon Nicholaides, *The Natural Way to Draw* pp. 9–14.

Eventually, you can develop more sophisticated distinctions—even with these primitive tools. Letting the stick dry out offers fainter lines that can yield a sense of the play of light. The drawing of the great hall at left uses dry lines to depict atmospheric perspective (the effect of atmosphere on the visual acuity of objects at various distances). Distant objects are drawn with softer lines, nearer ones with sharper lines.

Good contour lines are like well-told stories. Good storytellers know to vary the pace and level of detail of their narrative. At times they offer quick generalizations to set a context; at other times they hone in on the most precise descriptions of salient features or events. Inconsistency is at the heart of good storytelling. Nothing is more boring than a story that tells every little detail. Nothing is duller than one that offers only generalities. The trick is in the mix of detail and generalization. Sometimes you will want to labor

CONTOUR 4

Deriving perspective
<u>Conté crayon, newsprint</u>

ON
THE
CD

Now we begin to derive perspective. Don't think about convergence or foreshortening. Just focus on feeling the inclination contours take as you follow them in perspective. Pick a site with a variety of shapes and concentrations of detail. Your subject should have significant overlaps and a strong foreground.[7]

---

[7] Adapted from "Contour," in Kimon Nicholaides, *The Natural Way to Draw* pp. 9–14.

1.28 Above: See on demonstration CD.
1.29 Below left: Lexi Chung.

over an area in a drawing—exploring and offering up every detail. Sometimes you will want to skim along an edge. Vision, after all, is an uneven sense. We do not see all things equally at once. Our eyes scan the visual world restlessly searching out that information and those attributes, which are pertinent. We ignore the rest.

Are there some principles to follow? In general, yes. Profiles need greater weight, but not everywhere: more at tops and sides and less at bases. Vary profiles always. You need to constantly vary the character of your lines in response to what you are seeing. Think of lines in the spirit of Mohammed Ali's famous advice: "Float like a butterfly and sting like a bee." Let your line float like a butterfly when the information seems simple and unchanging and sting like a bee when it seems pertinent and grabs your attention.

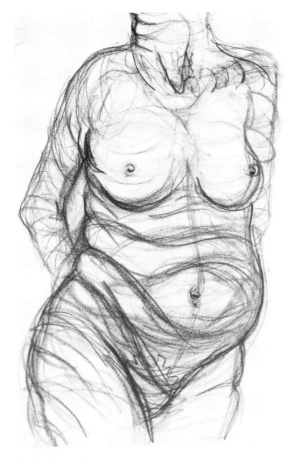

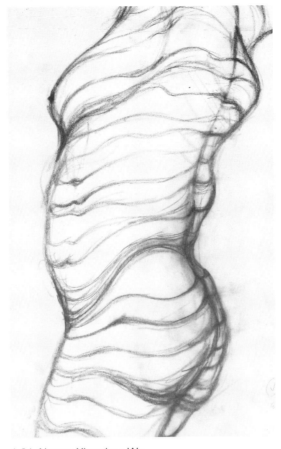

1.30 Misha Varshavsky.

1.31 Above: Xianghua Wu.
1.32 Below right: Rebecca Schultz.

CONTOUR 5
Wrapping the form
Felt-tipped pen, then switch to conté

Look at a point on the edge of the model where a significant cross contour seems readable; the waistline or abdomen is a good choice. Then from that location imagine wrapping a ball of string across the front and around the back of the model. Draw that string around and around the model.

After several drawings, switch to conté and show just the visible side. But retain a sense of the backside. When your line reaches a profile, hook the line just slightly behind the model. Your lines should feel as if they are embracing the form.[8]

[8] Adapted from "Cross Contours," in Kimon Nicholaides, *The Natural Way to Draw* pp. 20–22.

Cross contour

We've moved along surfaces. Now we'll move across them. Directed at mapping surface, cross contour drawing comes closest to the maps that interested Nicholaides in contour in the first place. The model's pose is key. One with shoulders rotated away from the angle of the waist makes cross contours more readable. Your location is also important. Sit close and low to the ground; look up at an angle. You want the sectional properties of the cross contours to be as clear as possible. To make their spatial orientation more readable, draw a line down the center of the stomach or spine. These lines help establish the twist of the pose and so clarify the shape of each contour in space. Though the exercise is not easy, these spatial reads will prepare you well for perspective drawing so long as you do not oversimplify contours.

CONTOUR 6

Drawing with straight lines only
Conté crayon, newsprint

ON THE CD

Now we will try to feel the spatial attitude of lines as we draw them. Draw as you have in previous contour exercises, but limit yourself only to straight lines. No curving lines are allowed! Hold the conté crayon between your thumb and forefinger. This grip will force you to sense a line's direction as you draw it: a key to sensing convergence.

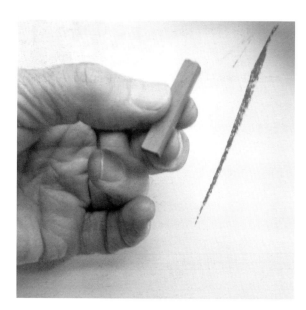

1.33 Hold the conté overhand, keep your wrist stiff, and draw with a slashing motion.

1.34 See on demonstration CD.

1.35 Coleman Rusnock.

Straight lines, the figure and perspective

As we move from free contours toward perspective drawing, we need an intermediate step. The straight-line contour exercise above offers a bridge between the looseness of free contours and the ordered convergence central to perspective. Stand up for this exercise and hold the conté with an overhand grip between your thumb and forefinger. Never hold it like a pencil! Keep your wrist somewhat stiff while you draw. Holding the conté in this manner will force a slashing motion with your whole arm as you draw each straight line. Drawing with your whole arm is to be welcomed. In keeping with the *transactionalist* understanding of perception, it will help you sense the directionality of the marks as you make them with your whole body—not just your fingers.

1.36 Brian Leet.

1.37 Vincent Chew.

Slashing lines and perspective

In using slashing lines for perspective drawing, our purpose is not to actually construct perspectives, but to sense their convergence: to feel it, and to imitate it. This exercise is athletic at its core. We are trying to derive perspective as a fact of the visual field and build a muscle memory of it with our hands and arms as we do so.

An architectural scene with numerous corners and a strong and well-articulated foreground is important. It should be one you can draw from a steep angle. Views from mezzanines or stairway landings are ideal. Pick stairs with strongly stated banisters and Newell posts. The slashing motion you make with your whole arm as you draw helps exaggerate your imitation of convergence.

Breadth of field, feeling perspective and being there

Sufficient breadth of field is important to feeling contours in perspective. Why? In an exhibition at Carnegie Museum in Pittsburgh, I once found the panoramic view below of Forbes Field, the one-time home of the Pittsburgh Pirates baseball team. It was taken from the right field stands during the opening game of the 1925 World Series between the Pirates and the Washington Senators. Partly because my father had attended this game, but also because of the photo's composition, I found myself coming to the Museum again and again just to see this view. The Museum kept a magnifying glass and portable steps nearby, and each time I climbed these so I could peer into the view from up close. It made me feel I was there at the game.

Obviously the photo's detail is important, but there's something more to it. This sense of being there arose because the view supports

1.38 Below: Forbes Field from the right field stands. 1925 World Series Game 1. Courtesy: Pittsburgh History and Landmarks Foundation.
1.39 Opposite above right: Wendy Wu.

multiple viewing directions. At the left we look down the aisle at the spectators standing by the column. (I eventually found my father in the fourth row from the top.) At the center we view the first pitch. At the right we look down over the stands. In the lower right, a fan can be seen sneaking a friend into the game by hoisting him up over the outside wall. Looking at the photo, I felt I was there at the game because I could look at it *as I would if I were there at the game.*

For this reason, push the breadth of field of your straight line drawings! The trick is to consciously develop two directions of view. The two views of stairs on the previous pages lead the eye straight-ahead and then up in the drawing on the left and down in the one on the right. Wendy's drawing on this page does a similar thing: leading the eye up and down stairs and along mezzanine balconies. And we, as viewers, feel we are there as a consequence.

CONTOUR AND COMPOSITION

Detachment and composition

With respect to the basics of contour views—how to think about them, how to make them—Nicholaides has written much. But what about their composition? He has written little on the subject. Because contours offer the key overlapping edges that are so critical to our perception of depth in the visual field, the subject of their composition has important implications for architectural design. We need to address it before moving to the more material and atmospheric properties of drawing, which are the focus of the next section.

A good place to start is where we began: with Nicholaides' deep distrust of vision and his sense that drawings gain strength when founded on the sense of touch rather than vision alone. At the outset, I had suggested that what is so suspicious about vision is its detachment: *we are here, and we are looking there, but we are not part of the situation where we are looking.* While this separation is precisely what is so useful about vision—the person sighting a mortar and lobbing shells does not, after all, want to be where the bombs land—it is separation nonetheless. And Nicholaides distrusted drawing for that reason alone.

Almost in an effort to salve Nicholaides' concerns about the drawings we make, we might ask: how might we compose views in a way that might lessen his sense that we are detached from what we are drawing?

1.40 Opposite: Douglas Cooper. *Holt and Barry Sts.* Heinz History Center Mural. 1992. Charcoal and acrylic on paper on canvas. 80" x 112".

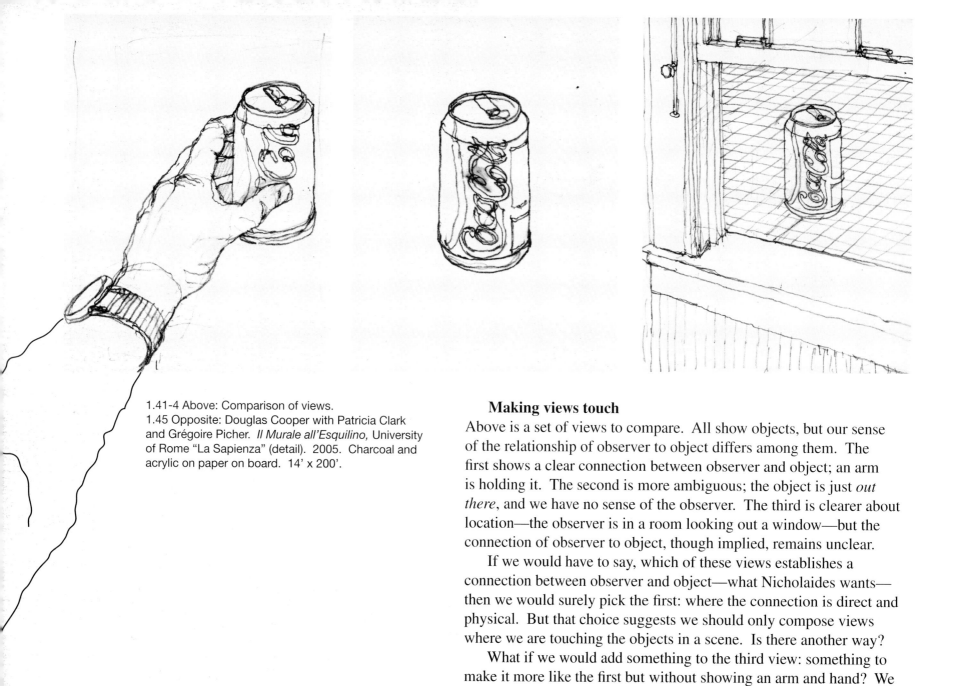

1.41-4 Above: Comparison of views.
1.45 Opposite: Douglas Cooper with Patricia Clark and Grégoire Picher. *Il Murale all'Esquilino,* University of Rome "La Sapienza" (detail). 2005. Charcoal and acrylic on paper on board. 14' x 200'.

Making views touch

Above is a set of views to compare. All show objects, but our sense of the relationship of observer to object differs among them. The first shows a clear connection between observer and object; an arm is holding it. The second is more ambiguous; the object is just *out there*, and we have no sense of the observer. The third is clearer about location—the observer is in a room looking out a window—but the connection of observer to object, though implied, remains unclear.

If we would have to say, which of these views establishes a connection between observer and object—what Nicholaides wants—then we would surely pick the first: where the connection is direct and physical. But that choice suggests we should only compose views where we are touching the objects in a scene. Is there another way?

What if we would add something to the third view: something to make it more like the first but without showing an arm and hand? We

might add a wing to show the observer is on the second-floor and use that wing to overlap the object. These additions would clarify where the object is, but without the observer having to touch it.

We should understand the significance of these additions in the kinesthetic and tactile way with which Nicholaides frames his entire approach to drawing. While it is true that the hand is no longer *actually* touching the object above, the eye is still able to touch it by extension. In a way that the hand and feet and body might follow—across the roof and down the column—the eye is still able to reach the object, after all. The eyes do the walking, and the view's composition provides the path.

In the detail at right from a mural at the University of Rome, we see a similar structure: The piazza and people provide the foreground; the street and distant bridge provide the path. The destination is St. Peters at the top.

A law for good composition

In making floor-to-ceiling murals for public venues, I have become keenly aware of the interplay between observer and scene. As in the Rome mural on the previous page and above, I have played a game of getting viewers to identify with a foreground place and then enter into the space of the mural along a visual path that I construct. I have come to think these three elements are necessary for well-composed views.

1) Views need foregrounds—like the train at left, they should leap out and grab you!

2) Views need routes the eye can travel—visual paths.

3) Views need destinations—places the eye can go.

But what about delight? There must be more to it than just establishing these three elements. There is in New Mexico a wonderful Christmas tradition. To light the way for the three kings to visit the newborn Christ child, *luminarias*—candles in small translucent bags—are laid out every few yards along the roads across the barren desert landscape. And in the cool winter night, one feels a rare connection with the surroundings. From foreground to background, the eye is led by these candle-lighted contours, point by point, out across the landscape and into every town. This is vision made connected in a way that would not merely satisfy Nicholaides but delight him too. Compose your views thus. Connect viewers to the world with equal magic! A gallery of views follows.

1.46 Opposite: The foreground should leap out and grab you. Approaching Train. Photo: Sarah Cooper.
1.47 Above: Douglas Cooper with Patricia Clark and Grégoire Picher. *Il Murale all'Esquilino,* University of Rome "La Sapienza" (detail). 2005. Charcoal and acrylic on paper on board. 14' x 200'.

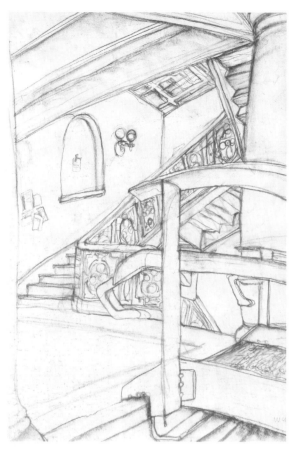

1.48 Above: Xianghua Wu.
1.49 Above right: Douglas Cooper. *Trash Day,* 1997.
36" x 48". Charcoal on paper on board.
1.50 Below left: Louisa Jauregui.
1.51 Below right: Ken Lau.

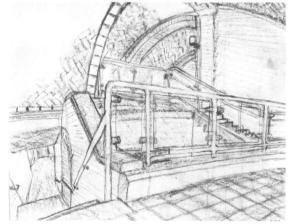

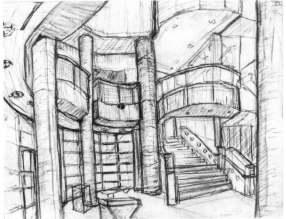

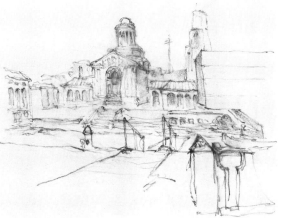

1.52 Above left: Douglas Cooper. *Route 30 to the Westinghouse Bridge*, 1998. Charcoal on paper on board. 36" x 48". (Private collection)
1.53 Above right: Patricia Clark.
1.54 Below left: Henry Huang.
1.55 Below right: *Hamershlag Hall*.

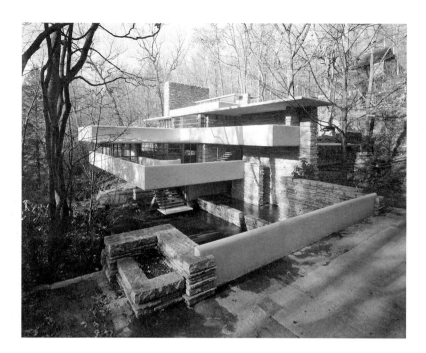

1.56 The eye is lead along a zig-zag path from foreground into background. Edgar Kaufmann residence (Fallingwater); Bear Run, PA, 1937. Photo: Bill Hedrich, Hedrich-Blessing. Courtesy: Chicago Historical Society.
1.57 Fallingwater, Frank Lloyd Wright, 1937, drawing after original rendering by Frank Lloyd Wright.

Architecture, contour, and composition

Among modern architects, Frank Lloyd Wright provides some of the best examples of the rule I just established that well-composed views shall have well-defined foregrounds and delightful paths for the eyes. Beginning with the low roof lines of his prairie-style architecture in Chicago in the 20th Century's first decade (the Robie House would be a good example), Wright became a master of zig-zag two-point perspective paths leading the eye playfully off into the background.

Perhaps the finest example of this effect is Fallingwater, Wright's masterpiece near Pittsburgh. In Figure 1.56, the foreground is the bridge, and the zig-zag path of the cantilevers leads the eye up into the woods or alternatively to the falls. In Figure 1.57, the foreground is the rocks and the falls themselves, and the overhanging terraces lead the eye on up the hill.

More recently the Koch Science Center at Deerfield Academy in Deerfield, Massachussets, shows just how delightful well-articulated contours can be. From the

1.58-1.59 Koch Science Center, Deerfield
Academy, Deerfield, MA. SOM: Roger Duffy with
James Turrell lighting design.

earliest meetings on the project, Roger Duffy, head of the studio at SOM responsible for this work, collaborated with light-artist James Turrell on the lighting design. What emerged is a lighting program that supports circulation and resonates the building's focus on astronomy. Like lead dancers guiding partners across ballroom floors, ceiling-mounted light bands parallel masonry walls and pull the eye along corridors, up stairs and into major public spaces. In the circular central lobby space, contours offer a more poetic content (above right): swirling with a sense of the cosmos and aligning with galactic orbits over a starry floor.

But what ultimately is the purpose of "good" visual composition? Returning for a moment to Nicholaides and to that point where we started Chapter 1, the purpose is not finally visual, but tactile. It is that sense of connection of our bodies—with our eyes serving as surrogates for our hands and feet—that sense of connection of our bodies to the vast surrounding world.

NICHOLAIDES AND MASS

Suspicions about appearance

In introducing the subject of mass in *The Natural Way to Draw,* Nicholaides decries a certain shallow and superficial sense of form that characterizes some drawings. To him such drawings miss essential properties of objects, and he points to instances of "cast iron clouds" and "balloon-like women" as examples. He goes on to explain that our first and most real sensation of many objects is of their "weight," something we usually gain by actually holding or hefting them. And almost as if we are engaged in just that, holding or hefting objects, he suggests that we should start a drawing by representing the weight of our subject. In this, much as we have already seen with his thoughts on contour and touch, here Nicholaides reveals once again a preference for the material properties of objects and a distrust of appearance. What lies behind his suspicion?

Background of these suspicions

Nicholaides was not the first to raise the issue. In the history of Western Art there is a long-running debate about the question of reality vs. appearance, and much of that debate casts doubt on the value of two-dimensional images. In a famous passage in *The Republic,* Plato dismisses the work of painters as lowlier even than that of common furniture makers. Plato considered working with concepts to be the highest and most *real* activity. To the extent that they depended upon the senses, he distrusted all other activities. But in this passage he showed particular contempt for painters. Even the furniture maker, Plato allowed, is at least making a *real* object—an instance of a concept and thus only one step removed. But as for the painter, not only does he work with an

---

[9] Plato, *The Republic,* in *The Dialogues of Plato,* translated into English by B. Jowett (New York: Random House, 1937), Book X, pp. 852–879.

1.60 Opposite: Sometimes our first most real sensation of things is of their weight. Carnegie Museum of Natural History, Pittsburgh, PA.

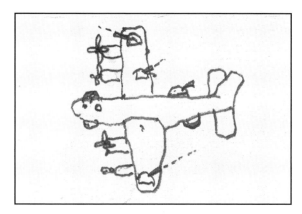

1.61 Toby's drawing: although it didn't look like a plane, at least it could fly. His had all the requisite parts.

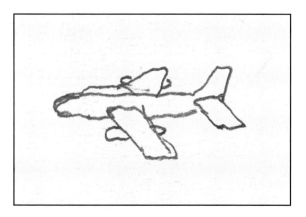

1.62 My plane looked like it was flying.

object, he limits himself to the appearance of a single aspect of it.[9]

Reading his words in *The Republic,* we even get the impression he believes there is something truly sinful about painting. (Once he characterizes painters as deceivers of children.)[10] But if we accept Plato on faith, even acknowledging that dealing with appearances is somehow suspect, how might we nudge painting and drawing a notch or two higher in Plato's eyes?

Thing vs. view

Years ago in a second-grade classroom, I got into a reality vs. appearance argument with my then-best friend, Toby McCarthy. The two of us had made drawings of military airplanes—this was during the Korean War—and I thought mine was better. His was drawn plan-like from above. All the parts were visible, and he was busy trying out various placements for gun turrets—on the sides, on top, and even on the wings. Mine was drawn in eye-level perspective from the side, with both wings foreshortened, and one wing partly obscured. In my memory my airplane really did appear to be flying.

Toby's argument was about function, and he was blunt. My plane had only one and one-half wings and one and one-half engines. His drawing might not look like an airplane in flight, but at least his could fly! Only his had the necessary parts. On and on the argument went from his desk at one end of the row to mine at the other.

Toby was emphasizing the "thingness" of his picture over its command of appearance. Could it be used as an airplane? Could it be flown? This is essentially the same argument as Nicholaides' with respect to mass. Although Nicholaides does not actually lay it out in this way, his comments have the same functional ring. Where Toby asked me to imagine flying my airplane (and his), Nicholaides asks us to imagine weighing our drawings.[11]

The more positive rating on Plato's scale, which I believe would be awarded to both Nicholaides' and Toby's interpretations, lies in their conception of a drawing as a thing in its own right. For both, making a drawing is more like the activity of Plato's furniture maker: more like making an object than making an appearance. At the heart of this conception is Nicholaides' exercise on weight.

Nicholaides' exercise on weight

With his exercise on weight, (called "mass" in this volume, see page 44), Nicholaides doesn't only ask us to weigh the object, he asks us to build it too, mark by mark upon the page. Consider how he starts us off. We are to imagine that we are drawing the core of our subject. Then, much like making a snowball, we are to pack material about that core, in back, to the sides and in front. In the end, these drawings achieve a heavy, brooding sense of weight that does not reflect the subject's appearance at all. But though they may not look like our subject, they are made like it!

Nicholaides' and Toby McCarthy's drawings suggest something very different from our common understanding of the relationship of a drawing to what is represented. With the word "drawing" we often mean—I believe mistakenly—a somewhat diminished second-hand version of the thing in the picture. This is hardly an adequate description for a drawing such as Toby's. After all, how many planes have you seen lately that have turrets on their wings?

What drawings must do

What then must a drawing do? What the real thing can do! but also more. It must not only be able to take the place of what it represents, it must empower us over it too. A drawing of an airplane must allow the construction of an airplane for those Toby McCarthys of the world who are too young (or too poor) to buy the parts. A plan drawing of a building must enable an architect to build, tear down, and rebuild (with graphite and paper) the interim trial solutions that a client could not afford to build if executed in real bricks and mortar. And a drawing of mass must allow us to build and shape the material of which an object is made. These are but some of the capacities that come naturally once we treat a drawing as the *real thing* and not a fake.

In the exercises that follow, we'll start with the mass exercise. Once we have the understanding in place that a drawing can represent real material, then we'll proceed in the more sculptural direction of modeling surfaces.

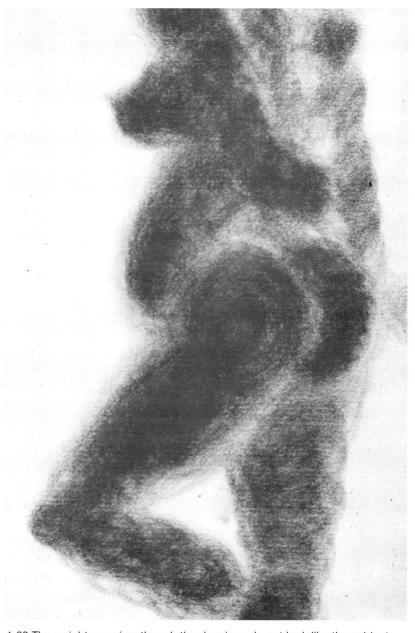

1.63 The weight exercise: though the drawings do not look like the subject, they are made like it. Unknown artist

---

[10] Plato, *Dialogues of Plato,* p. 855.

[11] This fuctional interpretation of Toby's drawing owes to E.H. Gombrich's brilliant essay, "Meditations on a Hobby Horse." E. H. Gombrich, *Art and Illusion,* 2d ed., Bollingen Series XXXV, No. 5 (Princeton: Princeton University Press, 1961), Chapter 3, pp. 93-115.

MASS 1
Massing with Conté Crayon
Conté crayon, bond paper.

Imagine the conté crayon is positioned at the model's center of gravity. Build mass out from that center: behind, below, to the sides, and in front of the center. Work as if packing snow about a snowball or layers of clay onto an armature. Keep building outward until you reach the surface of the model. When completed, your drawing should be dark where the model is thick and light where the model is thin.[12]

---

[12] Adapted from "Weight," in Kimon Nicholaides, *The Natural Way to Draw,* pp. 33–35.

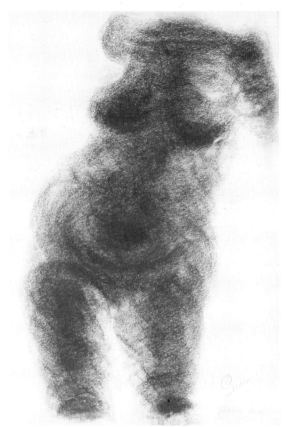

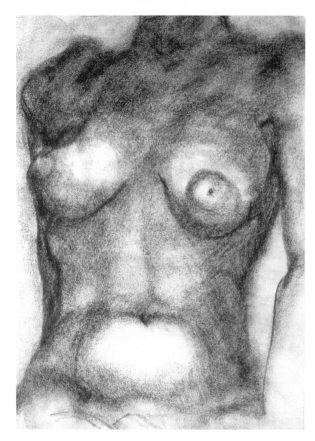

1.64 Above: Renee Yang.
1.65 Below left: Elizabeth Freed.

1.66 Kimberly Ruane Biagioli.

Mass and modeling

As was the case with your early contour drawings, don't worry about likeness with the mass and modeling exercises. Their value is the sense you feel of actually *making* an object while you draw. Differences among the mass drawings are interesting and reflect different approaches to making. The one above left is built from its center out. The one lower left is constructed more like a clay statue: limb by limb.

What is so compelling about the modeling exercise that follows is its parallel with the activity of actually modeling a real form. If you were working in clay, you would press the clay more firmly where its surface recedes. You do the same in this exercise. You press more forcefully into the page with the charcoal. There is an exact mechanical

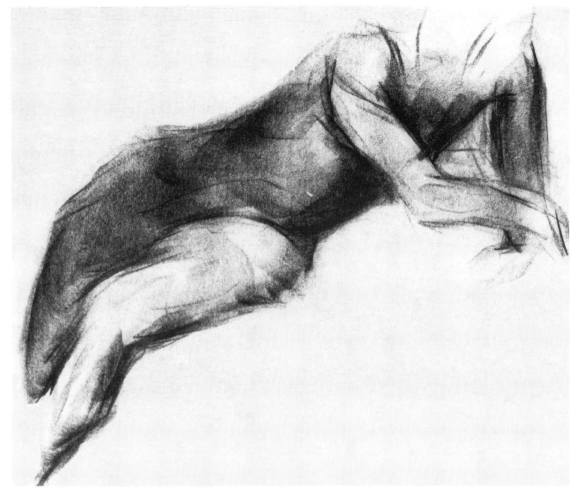

MASS 2
Modeling with Charcoal
<u>*Charcoal (soft Black), newsprint.*</u>

Build the figure's mass—as in Mass 1— but do so more rapidly and lightly than in that exercise. When you reach the surface of the figure, model that surface. Where the surface recedes, press the charcoal into the page. Where the surface moves forward, ease the pressure on the charcoal.[13]

---

[13] Adapted from "Modeled in Litho-Crayon," in Kimon Nicholaides, *The Natural Way to Draw,* pp. 36–39.

1.67 Above: Andrés Petruscak.
1.68 Below right: Frederique Turnier.

correspondence between the represented act of modeling and the real act itself.

As you work, consider your subject much as you would if you were making a sculptural relief. Focus more on reciprocal relationships among adjacent areas than on absolutist intent. You push one area back because it is further back, to be sure, but also because pushing it back will at the same time allow another area come forward. The drawing of the portal at right depresses the central area back not only because it is further back, but also because depressing it makes the flanking figures come forward as a result.

MASS 3
Modeling with Ink Scribble
<u>*Felt-tipped pen, newsprint.*</u>

Lightly build the mass of the figure with ink scribble (as you did in Mass 2). When you reach the surface of the figure, model that surface. Where the surface recedes, scribble more. Where the surface moves forward, scribble less.[14]

---

[14] Adapted from "Modeled in Ink," in Kimon Nicholaides, *The Natural Way to Draw,* pp. 51–52.

1.69 Above: Unknown artist.
1.70 Below left: Tammy Roy.

1.71 Unknown artist.

Progress

There is a big payoff to the modeling exercise. In the introduction I had described how progress in drawing rarely comes step-by-step: each day a little better than the previous one. Rather it comes in sudden spurts—and then often only after prolonged periods with little forward movement. A realization is made and suddenly the work is stronger. The *Modeling with Charcoal and Eraser* exercise is one where I frequently witness sudden forward shifts: sometimes even in dramatic fashion from one drawing to the next.

Maybe it's the opportunity it offers (what sculptor would not envy it?) for restoring additional material where material has just been sculpted away. To the right is one such instance. The drawings are taken from a single class. In drawing one Matsuro's understanding is weak, in drawing three it gets more resolute and by drawing four—note the flesh squeezed near the elbow in the detail—a truly sculptural feel is in place.

MASS 4
Modeling with Charcoal and Eraser
Charcoal, kneaded eraser, newsprint.

Using the side of the charcoal, cover your sheet with a general gray tone. Then use the kneaded eraser to pull some areas of the surface forward. From that point on, work back and forth: alternating pushing areas back with charcoal and pulling them forward with the eraser. [15]

[15] Adapted from "Modeled in Litho-Crayon," in Kimon Nicholaides, *The Natural Way to Draw*, pp. 36–39.

1.72 Xianghua Wu.

1.73 Above: Anne Riggs.
1.74-1.78 Below: Mitsuhiro Matsuura.

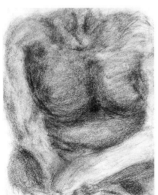

Implications for design drawings

In the exercises we have just completed on mass, Nicholaides framed the process in such a way that we believed the marks on the page were material. We built figures outward from their cores, and we slabbed muscles over bones much as we would if we were building clay statues. How might this understanding of drawing have an impact on the drawings that architects actually make when they design?

At the left is a developmental drawing from a series by the young German architect Thomas Spiegelhalter. He did them partly as life drawings—they started as drawings of machinery at gravel pits in Germany—and partly as exploratory drawings for proposals for works on that site.

What is important to observe in these drawings is how they are made. Much as Nicholaides' drawings of mass, these drawings have a compelling materiality. Building members are scribbled and smeared into existence and assembled in place on the page as objects. What we see here is not detached observation, but building in process. Later the impact of a similar order of assembly, first recorded at the gravel pit, emerges in the house shown below left, which Thomas designed for another location in Germany: a house made much as the original gravel pit drawing was.

1.79 Thomas Spiegelhalter.
1.80 Thomas Spiegelhalter.

When lines imply space
Conté crayon, newsprint.

Keeping the spirit of the previous mass exercises, use contour to define depth. At significant overlapping conditions, use lines to shear the visual field. As you draw, believe you are applying force to the page.

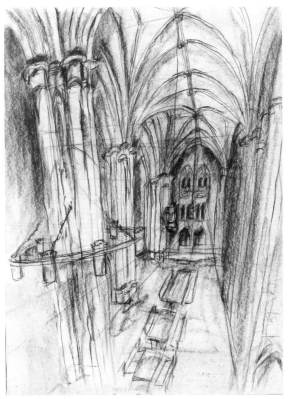

1.81 Above left: Yoonsun Yang.
1.82 Ken Lau.

When lines imply spaces

As we end this section on mass, I want to take us briefly back to our earlier work in contour. As different as those earlier contour exercises were from the recent ones we have done on mass, we can still combine the two. This is the intention of the exercise above—one that makes our line work sculptural and, in so doing, also anticipates upcoming work on volume. As you do this exercise, I want you to feel you are applying force to lines as you draw them: by pushing and pulling them. This is vision made forceful in its connection to a scene. You are drawing lines for objects, but at the same time you are acting upon the objects they represent.

NICHOLAIDES AND GESTURE

Learning by being

In the previous section, we considered drawing as a process of applying force upon objects in a scene. We sculpted them with line. This sense of drawing as a forceful activity has prepared us well for gesture drawing, a subject at the heart of Nicholaides' conception of drawing. Nicholaides wants our drawings to be active and alive. When we draw a boxer or a hitter in baseball, he wants us to feel the force of the punch or the swing. If it is fair to describe his approach to drawing so far as one where we have learned by doing and by making, then with gesture drawing he takes us one step further. We learn by being. We learn by imagining we are the boxer or the hitter and experiencing the same sensations they experience.

Static forces

The form, even of motionless objects, is a consequence of force. Their lack of motion indicates only that their present forces are in balance—not a lack of force. Words we use to describe posture are good indicators of this fact. Crouch, slouch and lean all describe motionless states; but they also characterize the unique muscular resolution of each stance. We see a poised cat or a coiled snake (or the camel and man pulling it in the cartoon at right) and feel an intense balance of forces despite their lack of actual motion.

The same is true of our perceptions of inanimate objects. We see a bridge across a gorge or a daring cantilever and use a word such as "leap" to describe how it spans the abyss or protrudes from the rock-face. The intent of gesture drawing is to give form to such insights.

1.84 We see an intense balance of forces despite the lack of motion. Cartoon by Willard Mullin, *New York World Telegram and Sun,* February 8, 1952. Courtesy: Shirley Mullin Rhodes.

1.83 Opposite: When we draw a boxer, he wants us to feel the force of the fighter's punch. George Bellows, *Stag at Sharkey's.* Lithograph. 19" x 24". The Butler Institute of American Art, Gift of Carl Dennison.

GESTURE 1
Feel and draw what the model is doing
Crayon or charcoal, newsprint

The model will take a series of quick, active poses lasting less than a minute. As the model holds the pose, let your crayon sweep freely and continuously around the paper. It should move rapidly and be driven by a sense of the forces present in the pose. Where an arm is held limp, let your lines also be limp. Where a foot is pushing off the floor, let your lines also push off the floor. Do not try to draw the appearance of the model. Rather, try to draw the activity of the model. Your hand and your lines should do what the model is doing.[17]

---

[17] Adapted from "Gesture," in Kimon Nicholaides, *The Natural Way to Draw,* pp. 14–20.

1.85 Jean Geiger and Albert Kim.

It relies on empathetic sensation, but empathetic sensation applied to things as well as people.[16] Like the great French engineer Gustav Eiffel in the 19th-century cartoon from *Punch* below right, as we draw something, we attempt to be that thing so we might feel what it is doing. Yes, when drawing a person who is leaning against a wall, we try to make our lines lean as well, but in addition, if we are drawing houses clinging to a hillside, then we make our lines cling to that hillside as well. If we are drawing the Hoover Dam holding back Lake Meade, then we make our lines hold back a wall of water! Gesture drawing is graphic statics.

---

[16] Empathy usually refers to a capacity to share the feelings of another person. I use it here to mean a capacity to share the physical sensation of another or, by transfer, of a thing. The word for empathy in German, *Einfühlen,* is instructive about the concept. It literally means feeling in or into another person.

1.86 If we are drawing houses clinging to a hillside, then we make our lines cling to the hillside as well. Douglas Cooper. *Morning Arrivals at Turtle Creek,* (detail) 1999. Charcoal on paper on board (private collection).

1.87 Empathetic sensation is feeling the same sensation as that thing. *Eiffel as the Tower.* After a drawing from *Punch* (1889).

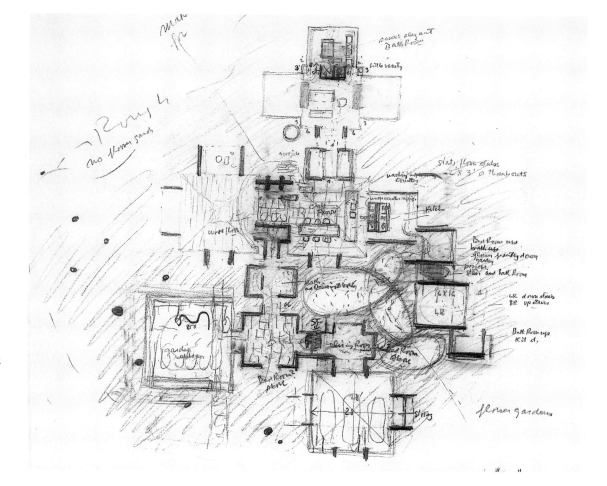

1.88 Right: Louis I. Kahn. Plan for Morris House. Louis I. Kahn Collection, University of Pennsylvania and the Pennsylvania Historical and Museum Commission.
1.89 Below: The locomotive seems to leap out of the page. The Broadway Limited circa 1938.
1.90 Opposite: Gesture drawing applied to buildings. Matthew Scarlett.

Gesture in practice

In architectural practice, the most important application of gesture drawing is in making quick diagrammatic plans of buildings. As in the plan view above of the Morris house by Louis Kahn, what the drawing shares with the figures on the previous page is the intention to express essential properties in a few quick lines.

Product designers frequently use quick gesture sketches to capture the "posture" of an object such as a hair dryer, or in the case of a vehicle, the motion its form implies even while remaining stationary. Images of locomotives such as the one at left from the golden era of the streamliner, seem in their form (and expressive representation) to leap out of the page and down the track!

Transferring a sense of gesture into design drawing is a difficult but extremely necessary objective—possibly the most important of all. Without this transfer, drawing can lapse into a lifeless process.

To assist this transfer for my students, I project slide images, so students can alternate figure drawings, drawings of expressive built works such as bridges, and plan drawings and elevations of the students' own in-progress design work. When no model is available, I use projected images of sculptural works—Bernini's work is perfect! One of these sequences appears above. Ultimately gesture drawing should infuse all your drawing, whether contour or mass or design drawing or even the upcoming work on volume, where we will be drawing literally nothing: the empty space between things.

GESTURE 2
Drawing what the model is doing.
Felt-tipped pen, typewriter paper
Using projected images in sequence, draw gestural studies of sculpture, built objects, and your own in-progress design work[18]

---

[18] Adapted from "Gesture," in Kimon Nicholaides, _The Natural Way to Draw,_ pp. 14–20.

SPACES AND VOIDS

Perceiving solids and voids

So far we've dealt with solid objects, and by now we have some sense about how we perceive them and might draw them. Solids are the material part of the world, the "stuff" of the environment. They are the parts we bump into and the things the radar bounces off. But what about the other part, the empty space? How do we perceive that, and how could we even begin to draw it? The answer is not obvious because empty space provides little to no sensation. It's empty.

I once lived in Siena, Italy, a city where buildings are closely packed and streets quite narrow—so narrow that I remember backing up flat against buildings when buses passed by. The streets are never straight, but are laid out to conform to level contours or follow the spines of Siena's multiple ridges and valleys. Nevertheless, though it lacks the familiar American grid, Siena seemed very readable. Most interestingly, the empty spaces, the streets and piazzas, seemed to have discernible shapes of their own. How did they?

1.91 Opposite: Cars on the Monongahela Warf. Photo: Clyde Hare, copyright © 1994.

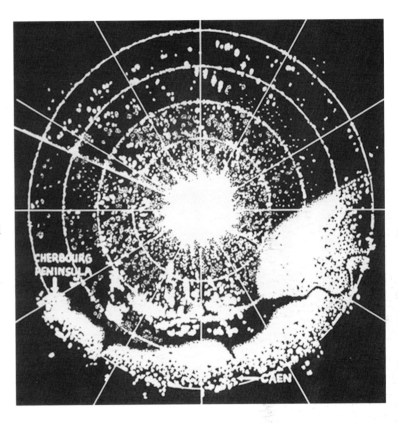

1.92 We cannot sense empty space; only the solids provide sensation. Solids are the part the radar bounces off. Radar view of the Normandy beaches on D-Day.

1.93 Where space is rarer it is also more compelling as a figural element. Plan of Siena.

One thing we can say immediately about space in Siena is that there's less of it. Owing to the close packing of the houses, empty space is a much more rare commodity than in a typical North American environment such as a suburban housing development or strip mall. In the United States empty space abounds. Most buildings are object-buildings made of relatively thin members such as wood, steel and pre-cast concrete. Our buildings tend to be free-standing on individual plots. There's lots of space between.

Looking at the plan of Siena and noticing how densely packed it is, we might state as a law of sorts that *where space is rare it tends to be more readable as space.* A narrow street in Siena with an 8-foot-wide bus racing toward us provides us with a spatial experience that is vivid indeed. On an American boulevard near a strip mall, that same bus would scarcely be cause for alarm. For similar reasons (rarity of space vs. prevalence of space) a mariner sailing through a narrow passage such as the Straits of Magellan proceeds with much greater caution than on the open ocean. In such tight situations, the dimensions of space are understood, even felt, because they simply must be attended to.

Nature is replete with circumstances where space is more rare and the solid more prevalent. Like the straits mentioned above, harbors, bays, sounds, channels, and seas are all conditions where a body of water is shaped by the surrounding and more prevalent dry land. Even more compelling, empty space takes on a particularly powerful read when we are also able to perceive it as the missing part of a solid. One reason the Grand Canyon inspires such awe is that we are still aware of the flat plateau that was once there.

Space as figure, space as matter

But while consideration of the relative rarity of space may help us understand the streets in Siena, what of the Piazzas? At times they are vast. The central Piazza, the *Campo,* measures some 500 feet across. But, readable it is—so readable that people often name it with comparative words. Germans call it *Der Muschelplatz* (the clam-shaped piazza). Americans compare it to a fan. It is interesting that both words refer to solids, and this fact is precisely the point. Where the shape of a space is so distinct that it can be compared to a solid, empty space takes on a peculiar quality. Though it cannot be sensed as a thing, we nevertheless understand it as a thing in its own right. In a true figure-ground reversal, we understand it as a solid's inverse.

There are other parallel and less architecturally charged conditions where we do in fact start to perceive the materiality of space as well. Think for a moment of a thick London fog or a summer downpour or a "white-out" during a winter snow squall. Under such conditions we do sense a material aspect to space. Its obscures our vision, or makes us wet, or pelts us!

These three conditions—space as the more rare element, space as figure and space as matter—point to ways to draw space. The trick is to find a subject to draw where space is well defined by surrounding solids and then draw it as if it were a solid. As in the sectional drawing of the building below, we flip what is our normal sense of things. We draw the space as the material part and the solids as immaterial.

1.94 Draw the space, not the solid. Sectional view. Rick Marron.
1.95 Where space is rarer and the solid more prevalent. Antilope Canyon near Lake Powell. Photo: Sarah Cooper.

SPACE 1
Deep-shallow
Ink, 1/4" brush, bond paper

Construct a still life that has interesting spaces between the solids. Bicycles, ladders and crates are good subjects. Then with brushed ink draw these "in-between" spaces.

1.96 Bill Birkholz.

1.97 Teri Tsang.

Drawing space as figure

The same three conditions just listed need to be kept in mind as you work on the exercises above. To make space the more natural figural element, pick a condition surrounded by large solid elements, and then compose your drawing so the viewer focuses on the space rather than the solid. Find a space with a compelling shape, and place it (rather than the solid) near the center of your composition. Remember our natural predisposition is to key on a solid. You have to actively counter this tendency.

To give space a more material quality, try techniques that activate it and avoid ones that are static. Don't begin by drawing the outlines of spaces first. Instead generate spaces outward from their centers and use a really active mark. Think of the action of your brush or pencil as analogous to the stick of a blind man probing a space. First center it in the empty space, then move it around the space until reaches its edges.

1.95 Brent Buck.

View a skeleton from a direction that has interesting and articulate spaces among the bones. Then with white-colored pencil draw these "in-between" spaces. Where the bones are found, leave the paper blank. Though it's more difficult, do not generate the voids by drawing their outlines first. Instead build them outward from their centers.

One of the more interesting intentions to pursue in the skeleton exercise above is to achieve a sense of multiple depths despite the drawing's limitation to only two variables: space or solid. The two examples shown here have taken very different approaches with this single intention. The one above draws two skeletons at different distances and uses the relative sizes of the spaces between the bones of the skeleton to establish depth.[19] The one at lower right, in an approach implying atmospheric perspective, defines the edges of nearer spaces more precisely than those of more distant spaces.[20]

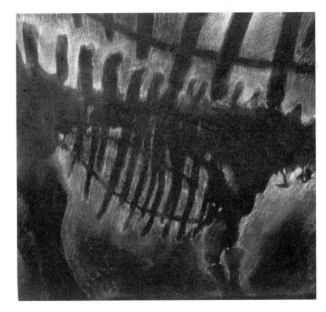

1.96 Neil Babra.

---

[19] Size perspective: a sense of depth arising in the relative projected sizes of objects of known size at various distances from the observer. See also page 107.
[20] Atmospheric perspective: the effect of air on the visual acuity of objects at various distances from the observer. Closer objects seem clearer. Further objects seem fuzzier. See also page 111.

SPACE 3

Deep, deeper, deepest.
Shallow, shallower, shallowest.
<u>*Conté crayon, newsprint.*</u>

While earlier exercises have certainly implied volume, by allowing atmospheric distinctions between deep and shallow, Space 3 supports a sense of actually occupying the depth of the spaces you draw. Enter a deep forest or plant conservatory. Find an array of foliage with well-articulated depth and interesting spaces between the leaves.

With tone, describe the spaces in between as deeper and shallower. Where the volume between you and the foliage is deeper, make your drawing darker; where it is shallower, make it lighter. Seek a murky and highly atmospheric sense of depth—like that of a foggy day.

1.101 Andrew Kitka.

1.100 Lyanne Schuster.

Drawing atmosphere

Where the skeleton drawings raise the issue of composition in a significant way, the exercise of drawing the spaces around an array of plants above is most of all about giving a material character to space. You have to think of space much as you would if the scene were filled with a thick fog, and you would proceed by drawing that fog. There are two obvious ways to start this exercise: with the spaces farthest away or with the closest spaces. However, I find it better to start with *the space* that seems the most prominent in giving the scene shape. This space may be closer or farther (more likely it's in the middle-ground), but its most important attribute is that it organizes and gives location to the scene's many sub-parts.

For the sense of *feeling* the space as you draw, it is important to work from the

1.102 Esther Chen.

1.103 Amanda Marsch.

1.104 Eliel Saarinen. Competition Drawing for the Chicago Tribune Tower competition, 1922. Courtesy: Chicago Tribune Company.

general to the specific. The small drawing at the lower left is only partly complete, and its history, from its earliest marks to its most complete state, is still evident. Note the area at its extreme left. This is how you should work at the start: vaguely and tentatively, always ready to modify shape and value as needed.

Volume is an elusive thing to capture. Drawing it requires that we attend more to the *stuff* between ourselves and the object we are drawing than to the thing we are drawing. What is required is a heightened sense of atmospheric perspective: one that activates the atmosphere. The drawing above right is from Eliel Saarinen's (1922) entry for the Chicago Tribune Tower competition. With the simple device of slanting lines, it effectively depicts the sense of sunlight streaming down on the atmosphere between the viewer and the tower.

SPACE 4
Volume and Orthographic Views
<u>*Ebony pencil, white prismacolor, chipboard*</u>

In this exercise we start from the middle and work both forward and back. From a neutral gray background, we depress areas (as we've done before), but now we also pull other areas forward.

With Ebony pencil and white prismacolor on a neutral gray background, draw an architectural elevation or section that shows depth defined by the openings and features of a wall. Darken those areas that are recessed. Use the gray paper for middle ground and for forward areas. Use the white more sparingly for forward areas, saving it for emphasis or, in a sectional view, for those areas that are cut through. Seek a highly atmospheric effect, one that represents the volume between you and the wall as much as the wall itself.

A note of caution: Although this kind of volumetric drawing does not *address illumination—it's about giving a material property to depth—because of its rendered appearance, it often gives the impression that it does. Do not conclude that it is always better to darken areas that are further from the viewer. Read the section on atmospheric perspective in the next chapter (page 111) for a fuller understanding of this issue.*

Working from a neutral background and group exercises

Other techniques can be used to represent volume. The exercise above uses a neutral background as a key element. Though it has the same objective as previous exercises, it represents space differently. Where previously you simply darkened areas that were farther away, here the drawing's initial state is neutral gray, and you use it as a middle ground. From there you operate in two directions—forward and back—using ebony pencil to depress some areas and the white prisma-color to pull others forward.

On occasion I have done this exercise as a group exercise. Students begin by laying

1.105 Façade of S. Gilles. First Year Group Project co-taught with Jill Watson. Class included: Hajime Ando, Nick Arauz, Lisa Aufman, Ben Bell, Colin Brice, Scott Chiang, Michael Gallin, Nicholas Hague, Kenneth Kim, Judy Lee, Peter McLaughlin, Alan Mizuki, Richard Monopoli, Michael O' Sullivan, Michael Parris, Basil Richardson, Sean Starkweather, Zaidi Tuah.

all the chipboard pieces on the floor and roughing in the location of major elements. Then they alternate working alone and mustering together as a group to consider the drawing as a whole. Much is gained from this choreography, for it closely parallels the thought process of an individual working alone—working from parts back to the whole— but it does so in a way that *physically* enacts this cognitive process.

Working as a group brings another important benefit. Students teach each other. By working next to stronger students and by trying to match the quality their work, weaker students improve, almost automatically. It is an enormous confidence builder for them!

SPACE 5
Sculpted design project
Carbon pencil on vellum.

In a full set of orthographic drawings, shows the space and volume of an architectural design project.

*   Note to instructor: It is best to conceive of this project from the start as one that is focused on volume, and to use some artificial means to this end. The design project shown above and at right used a ceramics cooperative for its program. It assumed a pre-existing limestone monolith 30' x 120' x 160' in a warehouse district in Los Angeles and the entire project was carved from that.*

A design project focusing on volume
From time to time, I have taught architectural design projects that have used the same volumetric representations as the previous exercises. Like those exercises, these projects treat volume as the figural element of the composition from the start. They foster understandings of plans, sections and elevations that goes beyond an understanding of a building's material. They address the building's space as well. In all of the projects, it has been assumed that the buildings are to be carved out or eroded out of a pre-existing monolith. I want to highlight several important characteristics of these projects.

Space is rare.
With the beginning condition of a monolith occupying the entire potential volume of the site, at the outset, solid material is maximized; it is everywhere. More importantly, empty space is minimized. It is nowhere to be found. This is the exact opposite of the beginning condition of most design problems. As a consequence, volumes are generated from the direction of their minimal possible sizes, rather than, as is normal, from their maximum. In this way it is easier to address the important question of the minimal volumes required for the activities within an architectural program.

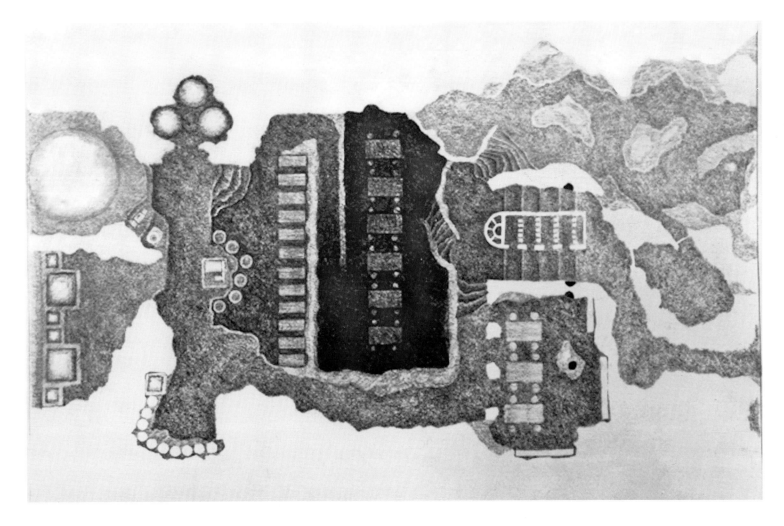

Volume is figure.

Since form is generated by making volume rather than by making material, volume naturally becomes the more obvious figure of the design. Likewise, the drawing process modeled in the design documents themselves remains analogous to the process of building that is presumed. The building would be sculpted; the drawing process models sculpting.

1.106–1.108 Ceramics Cooperative. Patrick Sutton.

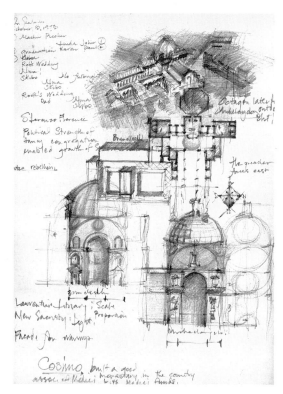

1.109 Notes from a class, Andrew Tesoro. 1975.

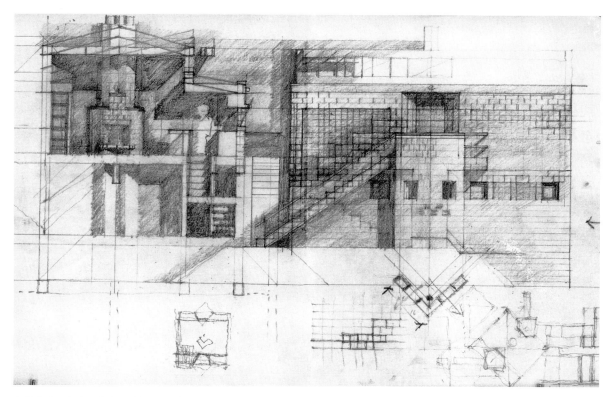

1.111 Study for Galeza House, Andrew Tesoro. 1985.

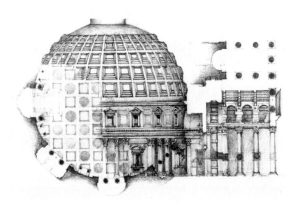

1.110 Plan and Section of the Pantheon. Andrew Tesoro. 1977.

Solid and void in practice.

The methods we have just used, which are related to methods commonly used by Beaux Arts architects of the late-19th and early-20th centuries, are still used by some architects today. My good friend, New York architect Andrew Tesoro, has long made use of drawings that show space as a figural element of design. Drawings he completed as notes in an architecture history lecture course (Figure 1.109) show this early fascination. Later travel sketches, such as that of the superimposed plan and section of the Pantheon, carried this understanding further. As a practitioner today, he often makes drawings such as the one shown above as part of his design process to represent the spatial implications of a proposal, even as he accounts in other drawings for the material facts of what he is proposing.

One of the most interesting contemporary works I have seen, for its dynamic interrelationship between solid and void, is the Korean Presbyterian Church near Detroit,

1.112 Korean Presbyterian Church of Metropolitan Detroit, Southfield, MI, Zago Architecture. Photo: Balthazar Korab.

1.113 Model. Photo: Zago Architecture.

1.114 Photo: Balthazar Korab.

Michigan, by architect Andrew Zago. Seen prominently through its transparent front tower/façade is a large red cross rising to a height of 25 feet. It nearly fills the tower void, and its arms extend outside the glass enclosure on either side. From outside we see the cross as an object. But upon entering the church our experience of the cross is transformed. As we move through the spaces between the cross and the side-walls, these "spaces between" become the more figural element of our experience. In a complex irony, by making the church's most dominant figural element—the cross—so large, Zago has reduced our ability on the inside to see it as an object at all.

Space and terrain

There is a way in which space can be drawn as a figural element, as we have just been doing, but in a manner that also addresses surface. We have already experienced this to a degree in the modeled charcoal drawings we did before. In our approach here, however, we will return to contour and contour maps, the topic with which we began Chapter 1.

SPACE 7
Drawing Terrain
Carbon pencil, coldpress illustration board.

Using carbon pencil on cold-press illustration board, develop a volumetric drawing that models the contours of a terrain.

Each fall, the first year design studio in Carnegie Mellon's architecture program undertakes a highly sculptural project in which students carve stacked terrain models. These models are carved from stacked and pre-glued laminated plywood constructions. In their early states, they embody pure stepped contours. As they are smoothed, their sense of contour progressively becomes more abstract, though it remains graphic on the models due to the darker and lighter alternating stripes of the plywood laminates.

The students then draw these models with tonal plans. As they draw, they try to do two things: 1) represent the act of carving by darkening those areas in the terrain that are deeper; and 2) represent the surface as a series of graded and stepped contours.

1.115 Puja Patel.

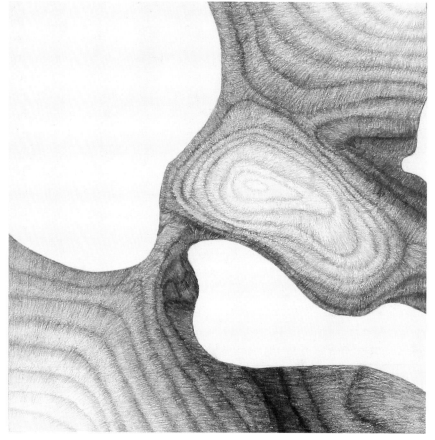

1.116 Diana Miller.

HOW DOES SURFACE RELATE TO VISION?

By drawing terrain as we close Chapter 1 we have come full circle back to where we began—to those topics that so interested Nicholaides in the first place: contour, surface contour, and the primacy of the sense of touch. However, in mapping the contours of a surface, we are also pointing in a new direction, one that is at the same time quite visual. What does our experience of surface have to do with our experience of vision?

I have offered some hints. Previously in relating surface contour to uses of decoration in architecture and product design, I have suggested that contours do in fact impart information to surfaces: information, which is quite visual. Examples of its use in architecture in the churches of Tuscany and more recently the work of Roger Duffy of SOM, demonstrate how what is fundamentally tactile can be the stuff of vision as well.

This issue, the relationship of surface to vision, will form the focus of Chapter 2. We will concentrate on the work of one perceptual psychologist, James J. Gibson. Unlike his predecessors, who had focused more on light and the conditions of the viewer in explaining visual perception, Gibson addressed the visual environment and the properties therein that give it order. Gibson found that visual order in the materiality of matter itself: in the visual patterns, which material surfaces provide. He believed that these material patterns form a pre-condition for vision—as important in essence as light itself.

The difference between what we have developed so far and what we will consider next —between Nicholaides and Gibson—is principally one of emphasis: the viewer vs. what is viewed. Whereas Nicholaides considered the interaction of an active viewer with the environment as the key issue of vision, Gibson, at least initially, focused on the inherent order of that environment. However, fundamentally there is no disagreement between the two. The work of both is rooted in a hard-headed focus on the materiality of the visual world. Even the words Gibson used for the visual patterns of the visual world, "textural gradient," are words loaded in their relationship to the sense of touch. Indeed, if he were ever asked, I suspect that Gibson (like Nicholaides) would have considered vision a derivative of touch. So as we move forward, consider what we will now address to be an extension of what we have considered so far: an extension of the sense of touch to the world of vision.

The Order of Appearance

GIBSON AND TEXTURAL GRADIENT

The ecological understanding

With the kinesthetic foundation of Chapter 1 firmly established, we now move to a more analytical approach to the question of appearance, one that like Nicholaides' pedagogy is fundamentally based on the sense of touch. While views on visual perception are numerous, this chapter rests on one: the early work of perceptual psychologist James J. Gibson as presented in his landmark first book, *The Perception of the Visual World.*[1]

Gibson, the leader of the so-called *ecological* view of perception, began his work during the early stages of World War II. He was contracted by the United States government to help in the development of what amounted to a forerunner of present-day flight simulators. Early in the war, many pilot trainees were crashing on their first flights. To better prepare them before putting them in the air, Gibson needed to gain a better understanding of the visual environment of flight they would encounter once aloft.

Though he would modify it considerably later on,[2] out of this early work on flight Gibson proposed a fundamentally new position with respect to visual perception. While not entirely discounting the roles of *predisposition* or *perceptual learning*,[3] Gibson argued that perception is based primarily on the structure of the environment. With respect to vision, he concluded that light enters our eyes in a state that is already ordered by the

---

[1] James J. Gibson, *The Perception of the Visual World* (Boston: Houghton Mifflin Co., 1950.), Chaps. 1–9.
[2] Gibson modified this view in two subsequent books. In *The Senses Considered as Perceptual Systems* (1966) he gave much greater emphasis to the contribution of both kinesthetic interaction with the environment and the interaction of the senses with each other. In *The Ecological Approach to Visual Perception* (1979) he emphasized motion parallax as the key characteristic of the optical array.
[3] Gestalt psychology emphasizes the role of predisposing laws governing the perception of form. Transactional psychology emphasizes the role of perceptual learning and interaction with the environment.

2.0 Overleaf: Douglas Cooper with Sarah Cooper, Rebecca Schultz, John Trivelli.
Mural: *New York, NY.* John's Pizzeria 44th St. 1997. 21' x 24'. Charcoal and acrylic on paper on board.
2.1 Opposite: Floor S. Maria Maggiore. Photo: Sarah Cooper.

2.2 Above: For Gibson the sensory data of the world already possess sufficient order such that perceiving can proceed on it alone.
2.3 Above right: Gibson found texture to be a natural condition of human inhabitation and behavior, even of matter itself. *Circle the Wagons,* Courtesy: Aerial Photos of New Jersey.

planes and surfaces from which it has been reflected. For Gibson the sensory data of the world already possess sufficient order such that perceiving can proceed on it alone.

This is an important consideration for architects and designers, and its importance goes beyond the fact that Gibson clarifies phenomena that are complicated and in dispute. Architects and designers must design for the general public. Insofar, they must presume the possibility of a spatial order that works for all. The central tenant of the *ecological* point of view, that sensation is in itself already ordered, is an absolutist argument. Its limitations not withstanding, it is valuable exactly because it is free from relativist individual and cultural concerns. As he proposes it, Gibson's order is universal, applicable for every time, for everyone, everywhere. What is the nature of the order that he found so compelling in the visual environment?

Gibson found that order in the visual textures of the world. Beginning with his wartime investigations of pilot disorientation during "whiteouts," Gibson came to believe that illumination is not the key issue for vision. Perception of surface is, and he came to believe that we perceive surface through the visual textures of which they are made.

Visual texture and textural gradient

For Gibson, "visual texture" became a broadly inclusive term. In *The Perception of the Visual World,* he includes artificial as well as natural textures, whether a floor of square tiles or a lawn of blades of grass. He includes textures at multiple scales, considering both the corn stalks of an individual field and the patchwork of farms that make up a mid-west landscape. He includes textures of all sorts of shapes and compositions, whether rectangular bricks in walls or round telephone poles in rows. Gibson finds texture to be a natural condition of human inhabitation and behavior, even of matter itself. Matter is made of discreet parts, and as such, it projects an image onto the retina that bears an ordinal[4] relationship to its parts. Made of discreet parts, the retinal image corresponds one-to-one with the material textures projected from the material world.

2.4 Made of discreet parts, the retinal image corresponds one-to-one with the textures of the material world. Italian shoe boxes. Photo: Sarah Cooper.

Gibson uses the term "textural gradient" to describe this correspondence between the pattern of the visual field and the world outside, and he uses it to explain how we perceive common conditions such as frontal and longitudinal surfaces, edges and corners. He explains these on the basis of the *signature* textural gradient of each condition. Frontal surfaces project uniform gradients. Longitudinal surfaces, surfaces such as floors and streets, project gradients that diminish with greater distance from the observer. Corners and edges project gradients that shift abruptly from the gradient in one orientation or distance to the gradient in another.

Gradients, depth cues and the exercises

The next pages present and illustrate the perception of various *signature* conditions in the visual world. These are followed by a series of exercises. The first explore the issue of texture, material and depth in a manner that is independent of linear perspective, in effect where Gibson began. Later exercises serve as a transition to introduce perspective.

---

[4] Having ordered intervals between stimuli.

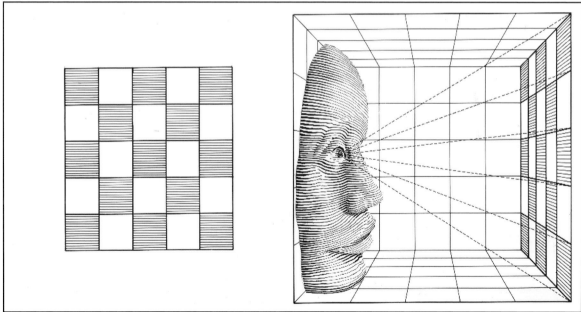

2.5-2.7 A flat frontal surface projects an array whose gradient (interval between stimuli) is constant. Top: wallpaper in Iceland. Photo: Sarah Cooper and Nina Gorfer. Left: Centre Pompidou (Beaubourg) Exterior of façade 1977, Renzo Piano (1937) and Richard Rogers. Photo: Eric Lessing/ Art Resource, NY.

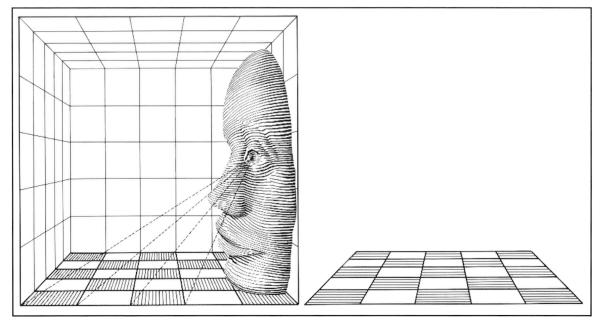

2.8-2.10 A flat longitudinal surface projects an array whose gradient decreases and nears the center of the retina with increasing distance from the observer. Top: Street paving. Photo: Raymond Mall. Right: Kakutobiishi (cut jumping stones). Enrindou (Enlin Chapel) Katsura Rikyu (Katsura Imperial Villa) 17th century. Japan. Photo: Steve Lee.

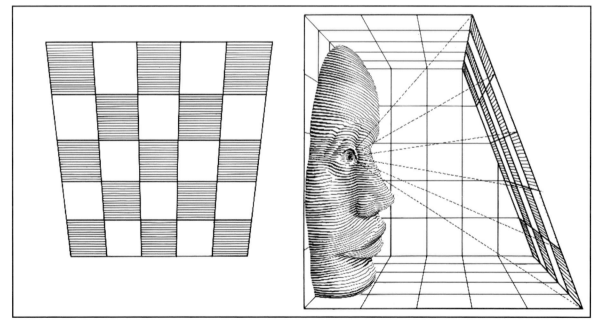

2.11-2.13 A flat slanting surface projects an array whose gradient decreases and nears the center of the retina either more or less rapidly than that of a longitudinal surface. Top: Figure at Zion. Photo: Sarah Cooper. Left: Grand Palace. Bangkok, Thailand.

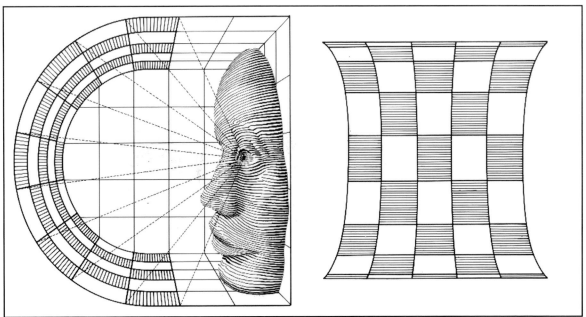

2.14-2.16 A rounded surface projects an array whose gradient changes from small to large to small as the surface curves from a longitudinal to a frontal and back to a longitudinal attitude relative to the observer. Top: Three Rivers Stadium. Right: Alcoa Building. Pittsburgh, PA.

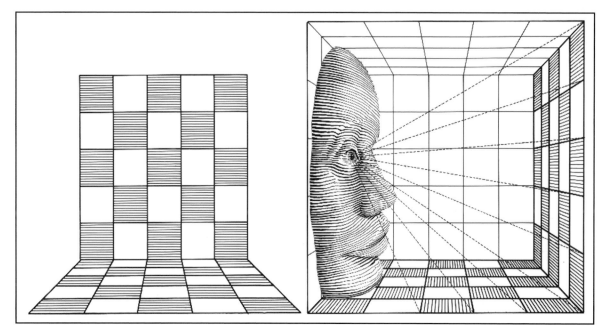

2.17-2.19 A corner of a surface projects an array whose gradient abruptly shifts from one corresponding to that surface in one attitude to one corresponding to that surface in another attitude. Top: S. Maria Maggiore. Photo: Sarah Cooper. Left: Gunma Museum of Fine Arts. Takasaki, Japan. Arata Isozaki. 1971 to 1974. Photo: Steve Lee.

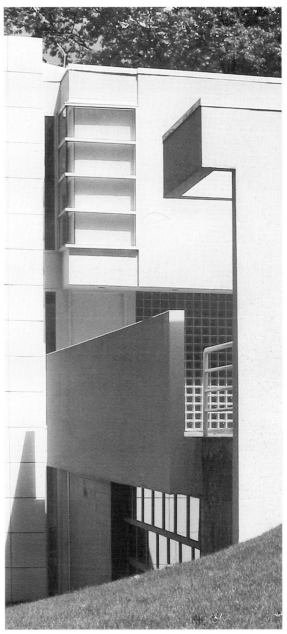

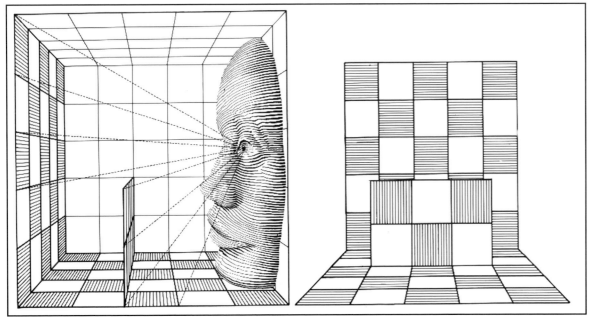

2.20-2.22 An edge between surfaces projects an array whose gradient abruptly shifts from one corresponding to that surface to one corresponding to the background surface. Top: Zebras. Carnegie Museum of Natural History, Pittsburgh, PA. Right: 18 Woodland Road. Pittsburgh, PA. Richard Meier and Associates.

TEXTURAL GRADIENT AND FORM 1
Organic form

Beginning with animal horns and later turning to more complex surfaces, conduct a study of interrelationships between surface texture and organic form.

2.24 Paula McLay.

2.23 Scot Wallace.

Textural gradient, touch, ornament, and architecture

Having considered signature textural gradients, it's time we address surface and vision together. As shown in exercises above, drawing organic form and highly ornamented buildings offers a rich mix of Nicholaides' pedagogy and Gibson's gradient. With organic forms, the material properties of surfaces—the way wolf fur falls, the way walrus fat folds—all provide rich sensory data for our sense of touch. At the same time, we must recognize the role vision plays in these readings. Where our hands and fingers can only move step-by-step along surfaces—they remain touching them—our eyes recognize patterns all at once and do so precisely because of their separation from the surface where they alight. This is vision's great contribution to perception. Touch is richly textured, but incremental. Vision is holistic and capable of multiple simultaneous readings.

2.25 Yoonsun Yang.

Find buildings with a high degree of repeated ornament. Use the repetition of these ornamental parts as a point of departure for reading convergence.

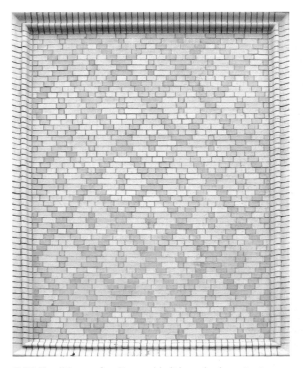

2.26 Traditions of patterned brickwork show textures at multiple scales. College of Fine Arts, Carnegie Mellon University. Pittsburgh, PA. Henry Hornbostel.

With ornamented buildings the issue becomes more complex. The essence of Gibson's textural gradient is repetition. One rose is not a texture; a bed of roses is. However, distance and size do play roles, and our perception of textures is not a constant as a result. Seen close up, bricks in a wall will appear as a texture. Seen further away, their texture may become altogether invisible. A central purpose of ornamental textures in buildings is to augment such conditions.

They do so by imparting multiple levels of information to surfaces. Traditions of patterned brickwork are among the richest architectural examples of surfaces in which pattern textures coexist at multiple sizes. In the image at right, the bricks exist as individual elements, but their variation in color also creates an overlaid diamond pattern that can be recognized at a greater distance as well.

TEXTURAL GRADIENT AND FORM 3
From texture to perspective

This exercise aims to derive perspective as a material fact of the visual field. We treat perspective as a special case of the textural gradient, one where material textures and repeated elements tend to recede to common vanishing points.

2.27 At the heart of ornament is the impulse to augment visual texture. College of Fine Arts, Carnegie Mellon University. Henry Hornbostel.

On complex surfaces, ornamental textures can add great richness to the articulation of surface. Henry Hornbostel's College of Fine Arts at Carnegie Mellon where I teach has a dense set of ceiling paintings over the groin-vaulted main entrance hall seen at left. These ceiling paintings have programmatic content to be sure—they depict the history of the arts—but they seem intended to do more than just that. They also make the ceiling itself profoundly readable. Note how the ornamental white edges between images radiate outward with the conical vault above the barrel vault at the base and then follow the curves of the groin vault. Like a *parterre* garden for the eyes, and for the eyes alone, the ceiling offers multiple paths that no hand or foot might reach—nor ever experience holistically if they could. Visual ornament makes touch sublime.

Owing to changes in material usages and construction techniques, contemporary uses of multiple surface patterns are often found at larger scales than bricks in a wall. Consider the façade of the Centre Georges Pompidou (above) by Richard Rogers and Renzo Piano, two architects deservedly known for their outstanding standards of craftsmanship. The façade has a recessed texture of window mullions and spandrels at one level, columns and beams with braced diagonal framing at a second (again as with the tradition of brickwork, we see a diamond overlay), and elements (often color coded) of building infrastructure, escalators and ducts, at a third. And we take this in all at once.

2.28 Opposite above: Xianghua Wu.
2.29 Contemporary material textures are often larger in scale. Centre Pompidou (Beaubourg) Exterior of façade 1977. Renzo Piano (1937) and Richard Rogers. Photo: Eric Lessing/ Art Resource, NY.

The Boston firm Office dA, led by principals Monica Ponce de Leon and Nader Tehrani, have made careful and exquisite use of material textures a hallmark of their firm's work. Some works, such as the Spiritual Center at Boston's Northeastern University, use contemporary materials. There they have surfaced the ceiling with polygonal metal panels that overlap and rotate around an oculus. The effect of a swirling cosmos of light overhead is as astonishingly beautiful as it is appropriate to the building's ecumenical use.

Another building, the Tongxian Gatehouse, near Beijing, China, uses traditional brick construction to such powerful effect that this ancient material almost seems reinvented in the process. In a way it's really quite simple. They have merely varied the depths of header bricks in a traditional Flemish bond to produce alternating highlights and shadows along a boldly cantilevered surface. There are two results. This highly extended and weighty edge seems lighter, and the brick texture, wrapping around the window, elegantly articulates the corner itself.

2.30-2.31 Opposite left and right: Inter-faith Spiritual Center. Boston, MA. Office dA. Photos: Dan Bibb.
2.32-2.33 Above left and right: Tongxian Gatehouse. Beijing, China. Office dA. Photos: Dan Bibb.

As we bring our introduction to Gibson to a conclusion, it is best to think of touch and vision—and all of the senses for that matter—as inseparable: one from the other. As we look at the astonishingly beautiful work of dA above, it is impossible to know (or even care) where the hand leaves off and the eye begins. To borrow (and slightly alter) a quote from Lou Kahn for a moment: to see is to touch beautifully and to touch is to see beautifully.[5] While Nicholaides was quite right to point out the limitations of vision, it was not so much vision he was addressing as vision without touch. While vision may have come from touch, the two do work hand in hand with each other. Gibson recognized as much. Increasingly as his career progressed and in particular in *The Senses Considered as Perceptual Systems*,[6] he considered all the senses as one.

[5] Lobell, John. *Between Silence and Light, Spirit in the Architecture of Louis I. Kahn,* (Boulder, Colorado: Shambhala Publications, Inc. 1979) pg. 8.
[6] James J. Gibson, *The Senses Considered as Perceptual Systems.* (Boston: Houghton Mifflin, 1966.)

GIBSON AND DEPTH CUES

Gibson bases cues on the environment

After presenting the role textural gradient plays in our perception of surfaces, corners and profiles (the building blocks of the visual field, so to speak), Gibson goes on to discuss depth cues. Depth cues are conditions of the visual field—one object overlapping another would be one—that commonly yield perceptions of depth. Though others had identified them before, Gibson contributed greatly to our understanding of their nature. What stands out in his explanation is the way it proceeds from his discussion of textural gradient. As was the case there, the characteristic conditions in the environment and their signature array of textural gradients remain central in his explanations.

As his predecessors had done, Gibson breaks the list of depth cues into two groups: primary cues and secondary cues. The first group, listing three cues, is dependent upon the existence of two eyes or upon subtle sensations of muscular response. They are effective within only short distances from the observer, and, because they are less involved with the conditions of the environment, for the purposes of Gibson's central argument (which is an argument about the environment), these cues are less important.

2.35 What stands out in Gibson's explanation of depth cues is that it proceeds from the textural gradient. Photo: Larry Rumbaugh.

2.34 Opposite: Depth cues are conditions in the environment that commonly yield a perception of depth. Working Partners. 1949 Pennsylvania Railroad calendar. Grif Teller.

Primary cues

1) Accommodation: based on the changing focal length required in focusing objects at various distances from the observer.

2) Disparity vision: based on the disparity of the views between the two eyes.

3) Convergence: based on the angle at which the eyes must converge in focusing on objects at various distances from the observer.

Secondary cues

The second group of seven, by far the more interesting as far as Gibson is concerned, had been treated as less important by those preceding him. Indeed, one of Gibson's great contributions is in upgrading the importance of these cues. Gibson's predecessors had treated them as a set of special cases that are learned. But Gibson explains them with the textural gradient, something that is not learned. He does consider them to be special cases as well, but for him they are special cases of the information from the environment, the continuous surface texture of the world around us. Thus he considers linear perspective as a special case arising when surfaces in the environmental have parallel alignments; and size perspective as a special case of the density of textures at various distances. For Gibson these cues arise as a natural correspondence between the retinal image and an environment made of discreet parts.

The secondary cues are the more interesting for our purposes as well because, except for motion parallax, they can all be replicated by drawing. They might even be called the "pictorial cues." I list them here in the order in which, in my observation, they are acquired as conventions

2.36 Gibson considers the secondary cues to be special cases of the conditions of the environment. Photo: Sarah Cooper.

for use in making drawings. This brief listing is followed with more lengthy explanations of each cue. These address two issues, the information signature and the use of the cue as a convention in drawing. The secondary cues are:

1) Distance from the horizon line: based on the tendency of objects to appear nearer the horizon line with greater distance from the observer.

2) Overlap: based on the tendency of near objects to overlap far objects.

3) Shade and shadow: based on three-dimensional modeling of objects in light, shade, and shadow.

4) Size perspective: based on the apparent reduction in size of objects with greater distance from the observer.

5) Atmospheric perspective: based on the effect of the atmosphere on the color and visual acuity of objects at various distances from the observer.

6) Linear perspective: based on the apparent convergence of parallel lines to common vanishing points with increasing distance from the observer.

7) Motion parallax: based on the apparent relative motions of objects at various distances from the observer when the observer is moving.

2.37 Linear perspective, overlap, and size perspective are all evident above. *Red Army* by Ray Smith.

1. DISTANCE FROM HORIZON LINE

Objects approach the horizon line with greater distance from the viewer.

Its signature

It is a fact of optics that objects seen in the foreground tend to overlap their backgrounds. The tops of trees overlap the background sky; columns overlap the ceiling they support; and tables overlap the floor on which they rest. And the positions where these objects appear to meet their background surfaces also indicate their distance from an observer. The base of a nearer column will appear lower against its background floor and further from the horizon line (the height of the viewer's eyes in the view). Conversely, the base of a more distant column will appear higher against the same floor, and thus nearer to the horizon line.

Its use in drawing

Distance from the horizon line first emerges as a cue pertaining to positions on ground surfaces *below* the horizon line. This fact owes to two characteristics of vision within our environment: 1) We live on the earth's surface, a condition dominated by gravity. Most things we see in daily life tend to be located on that ground surface, and logically we tend to think of their locations in terms of that ground surface. 2) We are upright beings and much of the time view the world from a relatively elevated standing position. From this point of view, most objects of interest appear arrayed against a background below the horizon line. Thus chairs, cars, houses and people usually appear located against the background of the floor or ground on which they rest.

Nearer Column

Farther Column

Horizon Line

Farther Column

Nearer Column

2.39 The base of the nearer column will appear lower in the visual field; the top of the nearer column will appear higher in the visual field.

2.38. Opposite: Above the horizon line, objects that are further are also closer to the horizon line. Street scene in Shanghai, China. Photo: Ted Anthony AP.

2.40 The cue, upward position in the visual field, tends to be used early in childhood drawings.

2.41 Upward position in the visual field is often at the heart of what we find so wonderful in the work of accomplished naïve painters. John Kane. ca. 1930. *Bloomfield Bridge.* Oil on canvas. 19-3/8" x 23-3/8". Carnegie Museum of Art, Pittsburgh. Gift of Mr. And Mrs. James J, Beal 81.54.2.

Upward position in the visual field

Owing to these characteristics of vision in our environment, when we make drawings, we can easily represent basic positional relationships merely by locating things higher on the ground if they are farther or lower if nearer. Often called *upward position in the visual field,* this practice of positioning things higher in the visual field to indicate greater pictorial depth is used by many cultures, even those that historically have not used perspective. In addition to *atmospheric perspective,* it is the central pictorial convention of Chinese and Japanese landscapes.

Perhaps because of its simplicity, this convention tends to be the first pictorial depth cue used by children. Children as young as age five commonly use it. All of us at around ages 5-7 have probably made drawings very much like the one to the upper left—with the road in the foreground, the house in the middle-ground and the distant mountain—all laid out such that higher in the picture indicates farther. *Upward position in the visual field* is often at the heart of what we find so wonderful in the work of accomplished naïve painters like the famous Pittsburgh primitive, John Kane. But this convention is not without its problems.

Difficulties with the convention

Though optically related to linear perspective, as the convention of choice of childhood drawings, *upward position in the visual field* later on seems to make some observations, which are necessary for mature perspective drawing, rather difficult to make. It is as if some vestige of this earlier convention makes the other more difficult to acquire.

I have had frequent exchanges like the following when I have offered comments on a student's perspective, like the one at right, which exaggerates the amount of visible floor surface in a view (compare it to the photo of the same space).

Doug: *"I think you're showing more floor surface than should be apparent."*

Student: *"But it's a deep space, and I wanted to make it look deep."*

Almost as a case of life imitating art, the observation seems distorted by the earlier use of *upward position in the visual field.* Greater depth seems to translate almost automatically into higher in the visual field.

Observations of overhead surfaces, surfaces above the horizon line such as ceilings, beams, and roof overhangs, are made particularly difficult by misunderstanding the convention, *upward position.* Above the horizon line, conditions reverse. Look at the view at the right. The nearer arch appears higher in the visual field, the farther arch lower.

Distance from the horizon line: a better way

Because of this confusion, the only unified way to understand how depth can be inferred from the position of objects on their backgrounds is to understand the cue in its relationship to the horizon line. Whether above or below the viewer's height, those things appearing closer to the horizon line are farther from the observer; those things farther from the horizon line are nearer to the observer.

2.42-2.43 Almost as a case of life imitating art, the observation seems distorted by the earlier use of upward position in the visual field. College of Fine Arts. Carnegie Mellon University.

2. OVERLAP (& MOTION PARALLAX)

Based on the tendency of near objects to overlap far objects.

Its signature

According to Gibson, readings of overlapping edges arise in abrupt shifts of textural gradient, from the gradient of the material in front to that of the material behind. Of the pictorial cues, *overlap* seems the most definitive. Though by no means foolproof,[7] an apparent overlap seems to establish exactly what is in front of what.

Edges and motion parallax

The reason overlaps seem so compelling owes to their relationship to *motion parallax.*[8] When we move, nearer things tend to move more rapidly across the visual field and distant things more slowly. Consider the view out the window of a moving car. Telephone poles beside the road whip quickly by; a barn on the other side of a field moves more slowly, and a distant hill slower still. Likewise, the textures of these various objects at various distances also slide at various rates of speed across our retinas. And it is at the edges of these objects that these various rates of optical motion unfold. In this sense, edges are where the visual action is!

Edges and the visual image

Not surprisingly, edges are those visual attributes we attend to most when forming visual images. Our gaze constantly roams the visual world seeking out pertinent information about objects and surfaces around us. But in forming the optical image, our eyes are

---

[7] Given a stationary viewer where gradients are not terribly obvious, readings of overlap function either according to prior knowledge of the shapes in the field or, lacking the former, according to the law of simplicity so valued by gestalt psychologists. Both of these processes can be easily tricked.

[8] Motion parallax: based on the apparent relative motions of objects at various distances from the observer when the observer is moving.

2.44 Opposite: Of the pictorial cues, overlap seems the most definitive.

2.45-2.46 The perception of overlapping edges arises in motion parallax: near objects move rapidly across the retina, farther objects more slowly.

also engaged in small involuntary scanning flutters (28 per second), called *saccadic* movements. At the edges of objects, this scanning yields information that is unique in the visual field. As our eyes scan back and forth across edges, the rods and cones on the retina receive information that oscillates back and forth, alternating between the information from the background to the information from the foreground object. Comparatively less information fluctuation attends those areas within objects or within uniform backgrounds. Changing information is always more important than unchanging information. Change can indicate something life-threatening or life-sustaining. So as might be expected, those areas (i.e., edges) where information changes the most are exactly those areas, which are more important in forming the retinal image. Like a squeaky wheel that gets attention, edges initiate the retinal image.

Its use in drawing

On the basis of *overlap,* flats in theater stage sets and paper cutouts in children's pop-up books produce convincing spatial representations. It is for the same reason—the optical action at profiles—that simple line drawings achieve such a potent sense of the visual field.

It should not seem surprising therefore that line drawing is one of the very first ways children use to represent objects. In the sense that a profile establishes where something is and where it is not, line drawing offers the immediate utility of objectifying things.

The visual field vs. the visual world

Odd as it might seem, in my observation young children do not use line drawings initially to establish visual overlaps. Indeed, they seem to avoid them at first. I once collected upwards of 100 drawings from an elementary school my children were attending. These were by children ages 6-8, and I recorded the children's ages as I collected them. I then tabulated their use of spatial cues in relation to their ages. They used *upward position in the visual field* often and early. But they used *overlap* infrequently and when at all, only when they were older. This was the case even among children whose drawings showed considerable skill in making lines. Why was this so?

2.47 Overlap is the reason pop-up books seem so compelling.
2.48 Many early childhood drawings do not use overlaps.

I believe there is an essential conflict between the two central intentions of line drawing: 1) objectifying a representation and 2) establishing spatial relationships, i.e., overlaps. The conflict is this: in the moment one object passes behind another, our sense of it as a separable object is lessened. Its recognizable profile is eclipsed, and it ceases to be an object to the extent that it was. It is a conflict that Gibson identifies in his distinction between the *visual world*—the objects and conditions out there in the world—and the *visual field* —the retinal image we use to record it.

The importance of line variation

It has occurred to me that this sense of a drawing—a drawing is an objective-representation-of-a-thing—may also remain a hurdle in mature contour drawing. How often have I noticed with contour drawing the difficulty novices have in moving away from an object's profile? Almost as a fixation, they tend to draw the profile and only the profile. Obviously for these older students, the intentions of drawing are quite different, but the formal problem of the inviolate edge seems the same.

There is therefore a paradox of sorts for line drawing, given what I believe to be its roots in overlap and motion parallax: reducing the overall dominance of the profile is key! A too-dominant profile flattens an image—much like the cutouts in the example of the pop-up books shown earlier. While convincing about position, such representations remain crude with respect to the three-dimensionality of any single object.

Earlier in discussing contour drawing in relationship to Nicholaides, I had urged you to willfully vary outside edges. It was for this reason, the tendency of uniform profiles to flatten objects— much like the paper cut-outs in pop-up books do. As an example of how to handle edges, note how beautifully Patricia varies edges in the drawing at the right. Sometimes the edges are strong; sometimes they are weak. Sometimes she leaves them out altogether and leaves us to infer them.

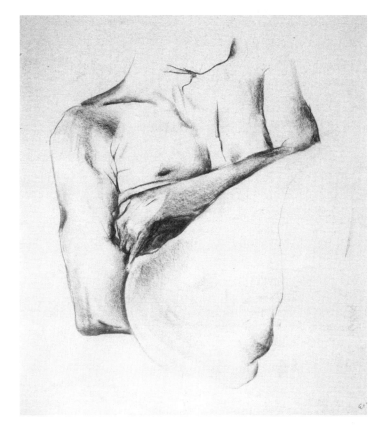

2.49 Overlap is the reason simple line drawings have such compelling three-dimensionality. Varying their edges will make them stronger still. Patricia Clark.

3. SHADE AND SHADOW (& DISPARITY VISION)
Based on 3D modeling of objects in light, shade, and shadow

Its signature
Gibson explains shading of objects in terms of densities of gradients on surfaces. Alone in his discussion of the secondary cues, his explanation of *shade and shadow* strikes me as somewhat obscure. But there is another explanation why *shades and shadows* seem to impart such convincing three-dimensionality to objects in the visual field. This explanation is independent of Gibson's textural gradient.

Relationship to disparity vision
Shade and shadow is related to *disparity vision.*[9] The basic information of the two cues is the same. They both depend upon the view from two distinct positions.

Disparity or *binocular vision* is the root of that wonderful toy of the 19th century, the stereoscope, that all of us have at some time experienced on visits to the eye doctor. We look through a viewer at two adjacent photographs that are slightly offset to differentiate the views from our two eyes, and *voila,* the scene seems real in a way that no single photo can match.

Disparity vision was also the basis for the commercially unsuccessful (and headache-inducing) 3D movies during the 1950s. I remember attending the "Charge at Feather River" (The Sioux vs. the Cavalry) sometime in the mid-50s and finding it absolutely necessary to duck the arrows that seemed to be fairly flying out of the screen. The fact is: *disparity vision* does provide a powerful sense of the third dimension. How?

Disparity vision allows us to see, however slightly, behind things. Each eye can verify just what it is that is being hidden from the view of the other eye. Almost as a reprise of *motion parallax,* the second eye sees just what would unfold behind the scene and at what rate if only we were able to move our point of view from the position of the one eye to that of the other. It is in effect *motion parallax* without the need of moving.

The comparison between *shade and shadow* and *disparity vision* is this. In the case of *disparity vision,* a second eye provides the second view. In the case of *shade*

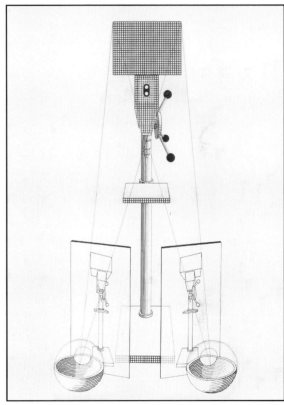

---

[9] Disparity vision: Perception of depth based on the difference in the view from the two eyes.

2.50 Opposite: A shadow is a picture from the point of view of the light source. Lake Powell Bridge. Photo: Sarah Cooper.

2.51-2.52 Above: The basic information of shade and shadow is the same as that for disparity vision; it provides information from a second point of view. Above: Stereoscopic image courtesy of Dr. Louis Goldszer. Below: Disparity vision.

2.53 Shade and shadow can indicate shape of what it is cast onto. Harvey Butts.

2.54 Shade and shadow can indicate surface relief.

and shadow, the sun or some other source of illumination provides the information of the second view. By indicating from the point of view of the sun exactly what would be overlapped, *shadow,* and what would be out of sight, *shade* (turned away from the viewer), it provides information that is every bit as potent as disparity vision. In fact, it is arguable that it is even more powerful. Under certain conditions—the sun at our backs and well to our left or right—the distance between the two sources and the resulting visual triangulation is great indeed.

How shade and shadow differ from each other

Shade and shadow each inform us differently. In general, shade provides information only about surface. Shadow provides information about both surface and location:

1) *Shade* can indicate shape: A gradual modeling from light to dark within a shaded surface indicates a rounded surface. An abrupt transition from light to dark indicates a faceted surface.

2) *Shade* can indicate surface orientation: The darkness of shading usually indicates the degree to which a surface is turned away from the light source.

3) *Shadow* can indicate surface quality and relief: A surface casting shade and shadow upon itself indicates roughness; a surface casting no shade and shadow upon itself indicates smoothness.

4) *Shadow* can indicate shape: The edge of a shadow forms a contour line on the object receiving the shadow. The shape of that contour line gives information about both the form of the object casting the shadow and the object receiving it. A serrated knife casts a serrated shadow. A Newell post casts a shadow on a stair that steps up with each stair.

5) *Shadow* can indicate the relative position of objects: An object that touches the shadow it casts is also standing on that surface receiving the shadow. A man on the ground will also touch his own shadow. A leaping man will not.

The power of shadow and light

Beyond their content as a cue of depth, shadows also imply the source of light: a lamp, a candle, or the sun. That source and even the object casting a shadow may remain hidden—often to powerful emotional effect. Masters of cinematic effect such as Alfred Hitchcock have used cast light and shadow from unseen sources to establish mood or even foreshadow future events.

Shadow and light present a compelling pair. For years I have drawn murals of my hometown, Pittsburgh. I show the city as I remember it from my childhood: when it was the steel-making industrial heart of the United States. Though the land was savaged, images of the poured slag rolling down the hillsides and the light flaring out as the Bessemers were turned still thrill my imagination.

In fact, the duality of shadow and light goes back to the earliest visions of mankind. In Genesis it is written: "In the beginning there was light." Proponents of the big bang theory write that at the outset there was light and that the universe and the Earth itself cooled out of the primal bang. Material is congealed light. Material and its twin, shadow, form a paired opposite with light. The one comes from the other.

Among the great architects who have composed in light and shadow, few stand out so much as Lou Kahn. Kahn wrote with great passion of the duality between light and material, and he masterfully composed sequences that led occupants from space to space through his buildings. It is a sense of longing that leads them: as if back to a primal source. At the very least, his compositions are marvelous for their three-dimensionality: the shadows cast into their recesses rendering what the sun cannot see.

2.55 Below left: I have shown the city as I remember it from my childhood when it was the steel-making industrial heart of the United States. Douglas Cooper. *Morning Arrivals in Turtle Creek* (detail).
2.56 Below: It is a sense of longing that leads them. Assembly Building, Dacca Bangladesh, Louis I. Kahn.

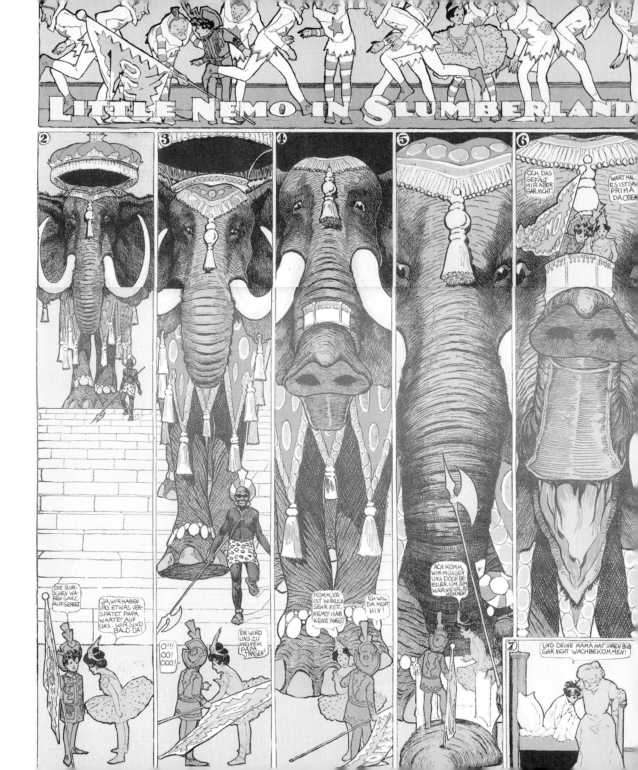

4. SIZE PERSPECTIVE

Apparent reduction in size of objects at a greater distance from the observer.

Its signature

Size perspective is based on the reduction of the projected sizes of objects and material textures with greater distance from the observer. It is optically related to *linear perspective*. Seen from the back of a train, the rails of a receding track converge into the distance. Likewise with greater distance from the observer, the projected width between the rails also gets narrower, the telephone poles shorter, and the cows beside the track smaller.

With the textural gradient, Gibson freed *size perspective* somewhat from the necessity of perceptual learning. Prior to him, it was thought to be conditional, requiring knowledge of the real sizes of the objects in a view in order to work. It was based on a comparison of sorts: a cow at a near distance vs. a cow at a greater distance; the cow occupying the greater amount of surface in the visual image must be nearer. But for the cue to work, we had to know something about cows. With the textural gradient, an attribute of matter itself, perceptual learning is less necessary. Though certainly helpful, it is not absolutely required.

I once saw an amusing demonstration of *size perspective* on "Sesame Street" that illustrates the point. In this sequence Grover came close to the camera and said, "near" and then ran off into the distance and said, "far." It was obvious to the viewer that the "nearer Grover" presented the larger image and the "farther Grover" the smaller. The sequence was skillfully presented, as I remember, so that no cues other than *size perspective* were in play. No ground surface was visible. Nor was there any scenery that would lend a sense of *linear perspective* to the view. Furthermore, the fact of the flat television screen framing the view made the differences in size between the two projected images all the more compelling.

It might be assumed from this illustration that *size perspective* would be dependent on knowing Grover. Certainly knowledge did help. But independent of knowing Grover, as he ran away, his material textures also got smaller. The yarn strands of his fur, his eyes, ears and mouth and the intervals between them all got smaller.

2.57 Opposite: Little Nemo in Slumberland. New York Herald Tribune, 20 May 1910, Windsor McKay.

2.58 The hand juts out like a well-thrown punch. Charles White (b.1918; American). *The Preacher.* 1952. Ink on cardboard, 21 3/8" x 29 3/8". Whitney Museum of American Art.

2.59 Foreground elements are enlarged. Samuel Rosenberg (1896–1972). *Monday Morning After the Night Shift.* 1935. Oil on canvas. 30" x 36". Courtesy of Arline Rosenberg.

Its use in drawing

One of the first images that inspired me to draw was the drawing from the fifties called *The Preacher* by Charles White, shown at left. With the preacher's arms and hands thrust forward at the listener and invoking the word of God, it is a powerful image—made all the more striking because White greatly exaggerates the projected sizes of the preacher's hands and forearms with the result that they jab out of the picture like a well-thrown punch!

One of the great mid-twentieth century painters of the Pittsburgh landscape was Samuel Rosenberg. Typical of Depression-era artists, he depicted the grim reality of daily life among the poor, and in a manner similar to White, he used exaggerated size perspective to pull viewers into his scenes. In the scene below left, note how the near building juts out with a greatly enlarged door and porch and how the figures in the foreground are oversized relative to those in the background.

Repetition is another typical element of *size perspective*. Whether by showing the same object at various distances or by presenting objects in rows as in Hopper's well-known painting of a service station, repetition of similar objects presents a powerful articulation of the depth in a scene.

Subtle uses of size perspective

These are some of the more general uses of *size perspective*: giving depth an extra push whether by exaggeration or skillful repetition. But command of *size perspective* can be subtle as well, in particular where other cues, notably *linear perspective*, are absent. Built on skillful representation of material textures, such uses build more directly on Gibson's great contribution to our understanding of this cue: its independence of prior knowledge.

Over a period of several months I once had an opportunity to watch two itinerant scene painters paint the background for a large diorama showing the African savanna at the Carnegie Museum of Natural History in Pittsburgh. The foreground and near ground were easy to depict. With stuffed animals, real bushes and tree trunks and then painted versions of same, there were lots of overlaps and ground positions with which to articulate depth. But the middle-ground and background had very nearly nothing—just bushes, grasses and a few overlapping ridges. Yet the savannah needed to appear to extend far out across a flat plain to distant mountains. *Size perspective* was really the only cue these painters had available to show that plain's compelling depth; and this was *size perspective* of a ticklish sort because the only thing whose sizes they could modulate were those small plants on the ground. How did they do it?

I went by one day to observe them at work, and I saw the wonderful trick they had developed. They had drawn a horizon line around the full circumference of the background painting. Pinned to this line at eye-level height, like so many garments hung on a clothesline, were human figures of all sizes. But while they were all different sizes, the proportions of these figures were carefully maintained. Then, day by day, plant by plant, at whatever height in the image they needed a bush or tuft of grass, they would simply dangle a human figure from the horizon line to that position on the ground. With the human figure, they had a ready proportioned scale and knew exactly how large to paint each bush.

2.60 Repetition is a typical element of size perspective. Edward Hopper (1882–1967). *Gas*. 1940. Oil on canvas. 26 1/4" x 14 1/4". Mrs. Simon Guggenheim Fund (577.1943). Museum of Modern Art. Licensed by Scala/Art.

2.61 The primary cue they could use was size perspective. Diorama, Carnegie Museum of Natural History.

5. ATMOSPHERIC PERSPECTIVE

Based on the effect of air on the color and visual acuity of objects at various distances from the observer.

Its signature

Of the pictorial cues, *atmospheric perspective* is the more painterly. Its information varies as a condition of the context, its atmospherics, rather than as an absolute condition of the objects in a scene. It arises in the fact that the light reflected from distant objects must pass through more atmosphere to reach the observer than the light reflected from nearer objects. There are two results:

1) *Distant objects appear bluer.* The materials of the intervening atmosphere (oxygen, water, and dust) tend to more effectively obscure the images of more distant objects, effectively supplanting them with their own reflected light, the blue color of our own familiar sky.[10]

2) *Distant objects appear less distinct.* In obscuring more distant objects, the intervening atmosphere is also intercepting the light reflected from those objects. The information from them is thus less complete. Less of it ever reaches the viewer. Bright surfaces appear grayer. Dark surfaces appear grayer. Sharp outline and detail are less crisp.

Its use in drawing

For centuries Western painters have mimicked the apparent "bluing" of distant objects by merely adding blue and reducing the saturation of local colors until objects acquire a soft blue-gray color in the distance. Fine Japanese screen paintings have traditionally used watercolor washes to deliver a soft atmospheric depth to their landscapes. But there are also ways of representing aerial effects in tonal drawing and even line drawing where color is absent. For drawing, the key issue is the reduction of visual acuity that occurs with greater viewing distance. Here are some tips:

1) *Use greater contrast of value for near objects.* In describing the play of light on

---

[10] So distinct is the effect of this apparent "bluing" that geographic features are sometimes named for it. These usually are mountains or mountain ridges that tend to be seen from a greater distance: the "Blue Ridge" of Virginia and Tennessee, and "Blue Mountain" in Pennsylvania.

2.62 Atmospheric perspective arises in the effects of the atmosphere on the visual acuity of a scene. Monongahela River Bridges, Photo: Clyde Hare, copyright © 1994.

2.63 With greater distance from the observer, brighter surfaces appear more gray, outlines and detail less distinct. George Caleb Bingham. *Fur Traders Descending the Missouri,* oil on canvas, The Metropolitan Museum of Art, Morris K. Jessup Fund, 1933. (33.61)

surfaces, give nearer areas greater range of value. In the foreground make things that are darker, very dark. Make things that are lighter, very light. Then, as things recede into the distance, reduce the range of contrast between these extremes, in effect approaching middle-gray in the distance.

2) *Include more detail for near objects.* The greater amount of surface area that nearer objects occupy in a scene (owing to size perspective) will quite naturally lead you to include more information about those nearer objects. More area available equals more information included. Push this possibility. Like a novelist depicting small but revealing details of a protagonist's behavior, focus in on the near objects in a scene. But be playful in this. Vision is not just near-sighted. There are also times when we suddenly notice details from across the room or way off in the distance. Include this sense as well, even as you acknowledge the greater visual availability of near ground areas.

3) *Use stronger lines in the foreground.* In an effort to make the foreground appear sharper, use heavier, darker and more precise lines for nearer objects. Lighten and soften lines as objects are farther away. But as in the above comment regarding the use of detail, do not be too uniform in your application. Playfulness is key!

4) *Find ways to represent the atmosphere.* As described above, *atmospheric perspective* arises in the effect of atmosphere on the visual acuity of distant objects. In effect, the intervening atmosphere covers them up. Try to show what it is that's covering them up: the rain, or dust or fog or snow that's in the way. An excellent example from the field of architecture of this usage is Eliel Saarinen's drawing of the Chicago Tribune Tower proposal (page 63). I include a painting here from a Pittsburgh colleague of mine, Jim Nelson, for its palpable representation of the near-blinding effect an atmosphere (in this case snow) can sometimes have.

2.64 Sometimes show the atmosphere itself. Jim Nelson. *Back to Pittsburgh.* Oil on canvas 62" x 84", Carnegie Museum of Art, Pittsburgh.

6. LINEAR PERSPECTIVE

Based on the apparent convergence of parallel lines to common vanishing points with increasing distance from the observer.

Its signature

Gibson finds perspective order in all environments, even those with no straight lines and little obvious perspective content. Seen through Gibson's "textural gradient glasses," clouds in the distance near the horizon evidence intervals of foreshortening that seem every bit as orderly as a grid of ceiling tiles. Indeed, the textural gradient is just that: the material textures of the visual world, natural or artificial, seen as perspective order.

On the other hand, *linear perspective* is a kind of special case of *perspective*. It arises in circumstances where objects evidence parallel lines—environments where a set of x,y,z, right angle coordinates is implied by the objects in the scene.

In Gibson's terms, *perspective* is a characteristic of the "visual field" rather than the "visual world." It approximates *how* we see, the retinal image, rather than *what* we see, the objects in the world before us. As a flat image, the painting at left shows tracks converging, one big train and one little train, and trapezoidal passenger cars. But that is not *what* we perceive. We perceive tracks extending into the distance, a near train and a far train, and rectangular passenger cars.

As with this view, the potency of perspectives arises in their ability to capture a visual moment in a way that is specific to one individual, in one position in space, and in one moment in time—a powerful immediacy. I confess that the train in this painting still seems to rush out of the page at me now, much as it did when I first saw this same view as a child of seven.

There has always been much debate about perspective along two sides. Is perspective a truth of vision? Is it evident to greater or lesser degrees in everyone's environment and a universal fact of the visual image? Gibson would certainly answer yes. He is prepared to find perspective in all places, even the grains of sand of a desert.

Or is perspective something that is learned? Is it a case of life imitating art? Does the world seem to converge only after we have first made lines vanish to common vanishing points? Is perspective, in other words, a cultural artifact, an issue for the vision and representations of some, but not others? The approach in the first chapter of this book,

2.66 Gibson is prepared to see perspective order even in clouds near the horizon. Photo: Sarah Cooper.

2.65 Opposite: *Spirit of America.* Pennsylvania Railroad calendar 1933. Grif Teller.

"Engaging the Visual World," aligns with this view. It presents the act of making marks as the initiator of drawing and by implication some aspects of seeing as well.

We shall come to no resolution of this debate here. The issue is also very much complicated by the fact that *how we see* and *how we represent what we see* are two very separate questions. For what it's worth, my own view takes a little from both sides. I think perspective is an absolute truth of the visual field, but only if we care to notice it. I have watched a sufficient number of students struggle with convergence to know that much about perspective must be learned. Be that as it may, this chapter does assume Gibson's views on perception. It will treat perspective as an absolute truth of the visual field. But first: some history of perspective.

Its use in drawing: a brief history through the early Renaissance

The history of perspective is an interesting story in itself, beginning with the Ancient Greeks and having an impact even to the present day on the ways in which we construct virtual worlds. This history would be outside the scope of this book were it not for the impact it so obviously has on Gibson's conception of the visual world and through that on the approach to drawing in this chapter. I present this history below to establish two understandings of perspective that are relevant to Gibson. 1) Perspective is based on an understanding of space that is universally applicable—x y z coordinates are extended everywhere. 2) Arising in that spatial conception, perspective makes the view of each individual predictable within that space.

The Ancient Greeks and Romans

The Ancient Greeks were the first to use perspective as a means to represent depth. In the 6th and 5th centuries B.C. their paintings of human figures evolved from a more rigid generic portrayal to one that used foreshortening and shading. They apparently reached a convincing level of "realism." Stories were told of Zeuxis who painted grapes of such realistic appearance that even the birds pecked at them, and of Parrhasios who painted drapes that caused people to try to draw them aside. It was also during the 5th century B.C. that the scene painter, Agatharchos, has been credited with inventing perspective.[11] Their knowledge appears to have been empirical. As far as is known, they did not construct lines to central vanishing points. But they did at least appear to understand and use a kind of general convergence to construct quite convincing stage set designs.

The Romans subsequently copied the techniques developed by the Greeks—many of their artisans were Greek. It is largely through their artifacts that we have knowledge of the Greeks' earlier command of perspective. Images unearthed at Pompeii and

2.67 *The Battle at Issus,* 2nd to 1st century B.C. Mosaic, 8' 11" x 16' 9-1/2". Museo Archeologico Nazionale, Naples, Italy. Alinari/Art Resource, NY.

Herculaneum in the 18th century show great understanding of both the convergence of parallel lines and the subtle foreshortening of human and animal forms. The mosaic above, a copy of a Greek painting and dated from between the 2nd and 1st century B.C., shows the Battle of Issus, Alexander the Great's victory over the Persians in 333 B.C.[12]

The scene presents the moment in which the tide of the battle turned, and Darius and the Persians began their flight. In the spirit of perspective, we have the feeling that we are there—the same immediacy of the moment that we recognize in the image of the train discussed earlier. The horses in the center and right are carefully foreshortened and racing along angular paths through the furious fight. Each combatant seems to occupy and defend a position on the battlefield.

Even more astonishing than the *Battle at Issus,* is a mural discovered in 1961 on the Palatine Hill in Rome in the "Room of the Masks" and dated possibly from the 1st century B.C. If we trace the convergence of the edges in this scene and examine

[11] Blanshard, Frances Bradshaw. *Retreat from Likeness in the Theory of Painting* (New York: Columbia University Press, 1949) p. 15.
[12] Honour, Hugh, and Fleming, John. *The Visual Arts: A History* (Englewood Cliffs, N.J.: Prentice-Hall Inc.,1982) pp. 146-153.

2.68 Wall painting "Room of the Masks."
2.69 Ambrogio Lorenzetti (1319-1374) *Allegory of Good Government: Effects of Good Government in the City* 1338-1339, Palazzo Pubblico, Siena, Italy. Scala Art Resource, NY.

its foreshortening, we see a command of these issues that is every bit the equal of the early Renaissance masters. Did these painters in the ancient world know what is called "artificial" perspective? Did they not just know how to make perspectives based on observation, but on knowledge of optical projection as well? With this mural we have to conclude that they may well have.[13]

For reasons that are unclear, perspective vanished from use as the Roman Empire gradually dissolved. The illusion of depth, so strong in the Roman images and even some early Christian images,[14] seemed to have been lost or become less necessary for the church and society as they subsequently developed.

Brunelleschi and the Renaissance Rediscovery of Perspective
Perspective first reemerged in the work of some of the so-called proto-Renaissance painters. In the years between 1250 and 1350, a kind of "stage set" perspective reminiscent of images from Pompeii is evident in a number of frescos: those in the Upper Chapel at Assisi (attributed to Cimabue) depicting the life of St. Francis, Giotto's frescos in the Arena Chapel at Padua, and Lorenzetti's large mural for Siena's Palazzo Publico (town hall), to name a few. In these images, parallel lines do seem to converge, though never to consistent single vanishing points. Their technique shows

receding lines slanting downward if they are above the horizon and upward if they are below the horizon.[15]

The first use of true convergent perspective is attributed to Brunelleschi sometime between 1416 and 1425,[16] and it is interesting that he used it as a simulation for a design proposal for the doors of the Baptistry in Florence. The first convergent perspective that still exists, *The Trinity*, was painted by Masaccio in 1425. It has been suggested that Brunelleschi showed him how to do it, but whatever the source, Masaccio's *Trinity* is the first post-Roman image we have that uses convergence to single vanishing points. Others soon followed: Paolo Uccello (1397–1475) and Piero della Francesca (1420?–1492) with paintings and Ghiberti (1378–1455) and Donatello (1386?–1466) with sculptural reliefs. Overnight, or so it must have seemed, the pictorial world had been remade.

How the World Seemed to Change

In his fascinating book, *The Renaissance Rediscovery of Linear Perspective*, Samuel Edgarton advances a provocative explanation of the nature of that change. As polar opposites about that change, he discusses two topographical views of Florence that roughly straddle 1425, the year of *The Trinity*.

---

[13] Wright, Lawrence. *Perspective on Perspective* (London, Boston, Melbourne and Henley: Routledge & Kegan Paul, 1983) p. 38.

[14] *The Good Shepherd,* a mosaic at the Mausoleum of Galla Placidia in Ravenna dated A.D. 425 is an example of a late Roman Christian image that still made significant use of pictorial cues of depth.

[15] White, John. *The Birth and Rebirth of Pictorial Space* (Boston: Boston Book and Art Shop, 1967) pp. 23–85.

[16] Though Brunelleschi's image no longer exists, his biographer, Manetti, gives a detailed account. Brunelleschi, the builder of the great cupola at S. Maria dei Fiori in Florence, had entered a competition for a new set of doors for the Baptistry opposite the church. He wanted to convince the reviewers that his proposal would be best, and he literally used mirrors. He positioned a mirror on the steps of S. Maria dei Fiori such that the Baptistry was visible. Facing the mirror, he created a kind of peep show demonstration. First he painted a perspective of the Baptistry with his proposed doors on a solid plate. Then he cut a hole through the back of the painting. He positioned the painting so the mirror was viewed through that hole and so that his image of the Baptistry with his proposed doors was exactly superimposed over the scene in the mirror. Though the methods Brunelleschi used to create the actual painting remain unclear, the fact of the peephole and its obvious equivalence to the station point used in perspective construction give this image credence as the first artificially created perspective. I have relied on three accounts : White, John. *The Birth and Rebirth of Pictorial Space* (Boston: Boston Book and Art Shop, 1967) pp. 112-121. Wright, Lawrence. *Perspective on Perspective* (London, Boston, Melbourne and Henley: Routledge & Kegan Paul, 1983) pp. 55-65. Edgarton, Samuel Y. Jr.. *The Renaissance Rediscovery of Linear Perspective* (New York: Basic Books, 1975.)

2.70 Masaccio (1401-1428) *The Holy Trinity with the Virgin,* S. Maria Novella, Florence, Italy. Alinari/Art Resource, N.Y.

2.71 *Bigallo Fresco,* Anonymous, 14th century.
Panorama of Florence, detail from the *Madonna della Misericordia* fresco. Loggia del bigallo, Florence, Italy. Orphanage of the Bigallo, Florence Italy. Alinari/Art Recource, NY.

The first view is a detail from a fresco at the Loggia del Bigallo painted in roughly 1350. The second is the *Map with a Chain* (named for its decorative chain border), a woodcut of the city from 1480. Edgarton points out that except for Brunelleschi's dome there had been few physical changes in the city in the interval between the views—nothing physical, in other words, that might explain the obvious differences between these two presentations of Florence.[17]

An inspection of the pictorial cues in the two views reveals just how deep these differences are. Both clearly do represent depth, but they use different cues to do it. Overlap seems to dominate the *Bigallo Fresco,* but it is not the sort of overlap that yields a clear read of objects at various distances. Rather, the buildings in the scene seem to rush out at the viewer all at once. *Upward position in the visual field* is also evident. Buildings lower in the picture are obviously nearer and the higher ones further. But because the ground is not visible—the view is simply too crowded—the view offers little sense of where buildings are relative to each other.

What does seem clear is our sense of the three-dimensionality of the buildings as individual parts (Edgarton uses the term "depth shape"). Most are rendered in shade, and the use of convergence at their tops seems to create a unique viewing angle for each.

By contrast, the *Map with a Chain* presents a readable and continuous ground. While it is not a linear perspective, the view uses *upward position in the visual field* and *size perspective* with such detailed command that we have a real sense of where important buildings are located relative to each other. And we know much of the city's layout as well. We know the city is built along both banks of the Arno. We know the Uffizi Palace is near the river and S. Maria dei Fiori farther away. And we could make similar positional statements about other buildings as well. Most important of all, because the background includes surrounding geographic features such as the mountains to the north and the hills to the south, we get a clear sense of where Florence is located in the world.

[17] Edgarton, Samuel Y. Jr. *The Renaissance Rediscovery of Linear Perspective* (New York: Basic Books, 1975).

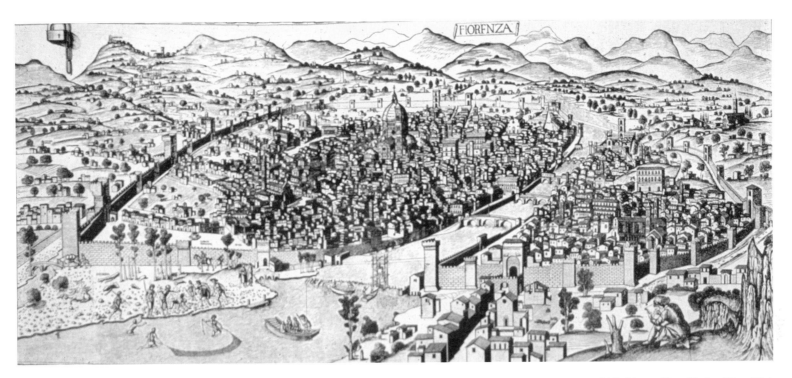

2.72 *Map with a Chain*. Alinari/Art
Recource, NY.

Does this mean that one view is more *real* than the other? Edgarton offers this
observation. Each portrays something real about Florence, but they show different
realities. The *Bigallo Fresco* presents the "feel" of the city: the visual excitement it might
have presented to an arriving visitor. The *Map with a Chain,* on the other hand, offers a
sense of overview, a sense of the order of the whole.

Then Edgarton asks a provocative question: With which sense of the world would
Columbus have ventured out across the Atlantic some 70 years after Brunelleschi in
1492? With that of the *Bigallo Fresco* or the *Map with a Chain*? With this question,
Edgarton suggests a deeper meaning of perspective, one that goes beyond its optics and
beyond its importance for making pictures. Perspective was, Edgarton suggests, a way
of ordering the world in xyz coordinates, a way that would be universal and applicable
everywhere. So useful would this spatial conception become that it would eventually
emerge in the gridwork of the Mercator maps of the 1600s that ordered the whole world
and made navigation to distant lands routine. Gibson would have felt at home in such a
spatial conception. It is the one from which his own understanding sprang.

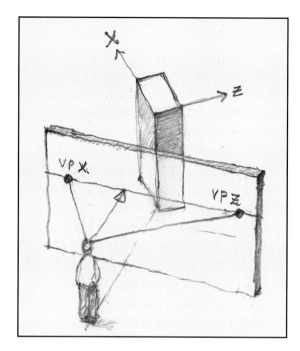

2.73 The relationship between the picture plane, viewing angle and vanishing points.

2.74 Use doubling and halving intervals to generate correct intervals of foreshortening.

Picture planes, vanishing points and such: from armature to view [18]
In the spirit of Gibson, we will now draw spaces with implicit perspective order. But in the spirit of the Renaissance and Mercator's maps we will extend geometry into what we draw by using a spatial armature. The key to its construction will be noticing the geometry the architecture already offers and using these steps and understandings.

Picture planes: The first step is generating what we call a picture plane. Think of it as equivalent to a sheet of glass perpendicular to your viewing direction. Where you locate it relative to your subject determines how you use it. If you place it in front of the subject, you use it as a window and view the scene through it. If you place it in back of the subject, you use it as a screen and project the image back to it in a manner similar to a movie projector. You use the picture plane to locate vanishing points, read convergences and measure apparent sizes: in effect, making these constructions directly on it. In the free-hand constructions you'll do in the next several pages, the generation of the picture plane is a simple step. In the one-point view, you merely use the end wall at the back of the space, and in the two-point view that follows you merely use a plane through a back corner.

Vanishing points: You begin the armature itself by finding the view's vanishing points on the picture plane. There is a general rule for finding them. For any set of parallel lines, you find the vanishing point by extending a line parallel to the set from your location out to a point of intersection with the picture plane. Put more simply, when drawing, just hold your arm parallel to the plane whose vanishing point you want to find, and your finger will point right at its vanishing point. Assuming a rectangular space, the locations of vanishing points and their number result from the direction of your view relative to the space. Looking parallel to the major axis of a space yields one vanishing point directly in front of you. Looking at an angle results in two: one for each spatial axis. In both cases, the vanishing points will be along the horizon line—a line drawn on the picture plane to represent the height of the viewer's location. After you've found the vanishing points, radiate

[18] Colleague Bruce Lindsey and his teacher Phil Grausman (Yale) contributed to my thinking on the geometric armature. See: Crit 15, *The Architectural Student Journal*, Summer 1985.

key alignments (such as beams and openings) out from the view's vanishing points.

Foreshortening: Represent foreshortening of intervals along the side surfaces in your space, the central issue of the armature, over the top of these radiating lines. There are two methods. Both are shown below left.

1) Halving intervals (left side): Guess one large interval with an even number of parts, e.g., four column bays. Using the diagonals of this interval, divide it into two halves. Using the same method continuously applied, subdivide these intervals into smaller units.

2) Doubling intervals (right side): Guess one small interval, e.g., one column bay. Find the mid-point of an opposite side. Extend a diagonal from one corner of the interval through that midpoint, thus doubling the original interval.

Hierarchy of lineweights: As you work over top of the armature, retain a hierarchy of line weights: heavier lines representing the architecture, and lighter lines the underlying geometric order. Styles in this treatment can vary widely. Above left the hierarchy is quite evident; above right the armature is only faintly visible.

FREEHAND PERSPECTIVE 1
One-point interior view

ON THE CD

Find a long space with well-articulated depth. Look parallel to its long axis at the end wall and draw its geometry. This end wall will serve as your picture plane. Locate that point on the end wall directly opposite you. Because you're looking parallel to the sidewalls of the space, this point will serve as the view's central vanishing point.

Through it draw the view's horizon line. Now pull the space forward. Radiate lines representing heights of openings, beams and other features out from the central vanishing point. Along a sidewall foreshorten intervals of depth; use one of the two methods shown on the previous page. Draw the perspective over the geometric armature you have created.

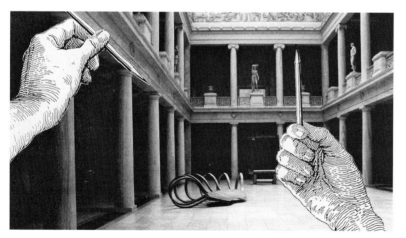

2.77 Above right: See on demonstration CD.
2.78 Above: Measuring projected angles and lengths.

Measure angles and distances on the picture plane: Remember that projected angles and lengths often differ from the actual angles and lengths of the objects you're drawing. What is in fact 90° probably will not project as 90° in the perspective; what is a square probably will not project as a square. Measure projected angles by using your pencil as a protractor of sorts: placing it over the optical angle, measuring it off a vertical or horizontal, and then transferring it to your drawing. To measure projected lengths, use your pencil as a ruler. Superimpose it over a distance already drawn in the scene, and use the comparison to transfer it correctly into your drawing.

Draw transparently: As you generate the underlying geometry of objects and conditions, draw them as wire frames. Treat the construction of their invisible faces as equally important to those you can see. Note in the drawing

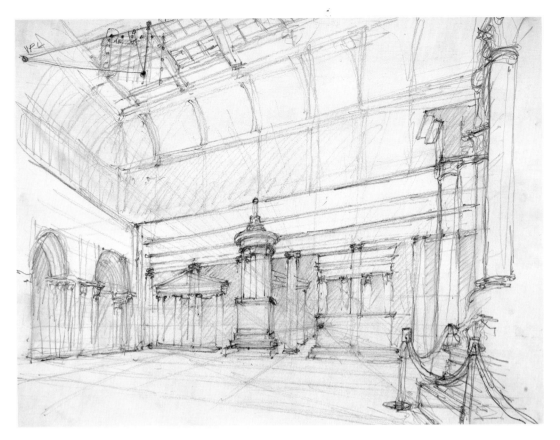

FREEHAND PERSPECTIVE 2
Two-point interior view

Draw a small plan of your space. In it represent your position, a viewing angle and a picture plane perpendicular to that viewing angle and through the back corner of the space. Begin the perspective by drawing a vertical line to represent the back corner of the space. At eye level draw the horizon line across this vertical. Along it locate vanishing points for the two spatial axes.

Draw lines in the plan, which are parallel to each spatial axis, to correctly reference the locations of vanishing points relative to the original corner: whether close in or far afield. Draw lines radiating out from the two vanishing points and use method of doubling or halving to extend the armature forward. Draw the perspective over the geometric armature you have created.

above left how I constructed the niches along the right side as if I could see right through them.

Construct the shapes you draw. Be attentive to their geometry and use what you know about them to draw them. As an example, when you draw circles, draw them as shapes inscribed into perspective squares. Draw their midlines and use these points of tangency to shape them. Such constructions have shaped the central and side arches of the space shown above left.

Draw a plan and set your view in it: To use freehand perspective as part of design process, ultimately you must be able to establish its relationship to the plan of the space you're drawing, and visualizing the location of vanishing points in that plan is the key. Do as I did in the drawing above. Draw a plan of the space, draw a picture plan and locate vanishing points along it.

2.79 Above left: See on demonstration CD.
2.80 Above: Xianghua Wu.

2.81 Jonathan Kline.
2.82 Right: Jared Langevin.

Issues of Style

There is no single way to build up lines over the top of the armature. The exercise examples I have shown so far have been precise in style and quite elaborate in detail, but I have chosen them only for didactic reasons: to clearly show process. They are not the only models to follow. Perspectives come in all styles reflecting their intent. At times as shown above left, they should remain relatively abstract. At other times as in the drawing immediately above, they might accurately (and elegantly) mimic appearance.

2.83 Wendy Wu.

At still other times they need to have the impulse of gesture. In such cases, though your understanding of the underlying construction needs to be precise and well practiced, do them quickly! As Wendy shows above, invest them once again with the feel of the exercises in Chapter 1. Ultimately speed is an essential issue. If you cannot draw perspectives quickly, you will not tend to use them as a tool in your design process.

FREEHAND PERSPECTIVE 3
One-point view of stairs

Begin by drawing the geometry of the back wall of the space occupied by the stair. Include the central vanishing point, horizon line, and heights and widths of landings and risers. Radiate lines pertinent to the stair's plan out from the central vanishing point.

In the perspective, project a plan of the stair forward from the back wall. Guess the depth of the back landing and generate the stair's run proportionally. Erect landings up from the plan. Erect verticals at the corners of the most forward stair and bring the height of the first stair forward from the back wall. Construct the first stair. To represent the stair's slope, draw diagonals on either side of the stair from the nose of the first stair up to the stair's landing. Use the heights of other risers brought forward to build the remaining stairs.

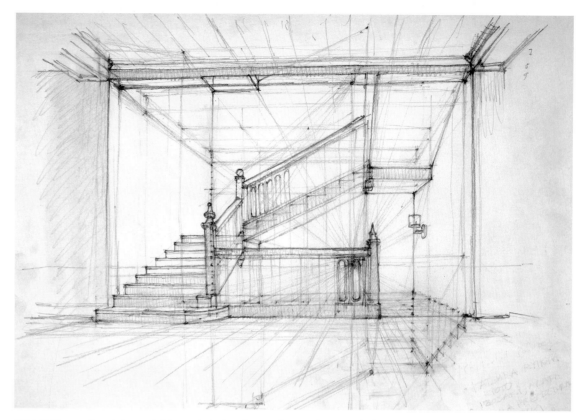

2.84-5 One-point stair: vanishing points for diagonals are above or below vanishing points for horizontals.

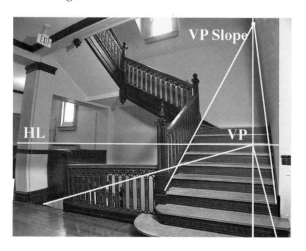

Drawing stairs

Now that you know how to use geometry to structure a perspective view, we can deal with a more difficult subject: stairs. No other architectural element so obviously addresses all three spatial axes. Furthermore, their sloping elements—banisters, stringers, etc.—offer ready demonstration of the more general issue of the location of vanishing points for slopes. This knowledge will help you draw slopes in the landscape.

To visualize a stair's vanishing point simply extend your arm and point your finger in a direction parallel to its slope. If the stair is sloping up away from you, its vanishing point will be high in the visual field. If the stair is sloping down away from you, its vanishing point will be low. Your finger will point to them. Furthermore, both these vanishing points will be directly above or below the central vanishing point for the stair's horizontal elements—its treads and landings—and,

2.86 See on demonstration CD.

Draw a small plan of your space in an upper corner of your sheet and represent your position, a viewing angle and a picture plane perpendicular to that viewing angle.

Start the perspective by drawing a major vertical corner of the space. Draw the horizon line and along it locate the view's two vanishing points. Draw lines radiating out from the two vanishing points.

Develop the plan of the stair forward. Guess the depth of the back landing and generate the depth of the stair's run as a proportion of it.

Erect landings up from the plan. Erect verticals at the corners of the most forward stair. Bring the height of the first stair forward from the back wall to construct the first stair. Draw diagonals on either side of the stair from the nose of the first stair up to the stair's landing. Use the heights of the other risers brought forward to these diagonals to build in other treads and risers.

assuming they slope at equal rates, they will also be equidistant from that central vanishing point.

In two-point views, the location of vanishing points for ascending or descending slopes is more complicated. These vanishing points will still be equidistant above or below the vanishing point for the axis they parallel, but the actual distance will vary with how far afield the plane's central vanishing point is located: whether near to the view's center or far from it.

Though stairways do not readily relate to plans of spaces, in drawing stairs it is best to start with a projected plan (in the view) of the space where the stair is positioned. The process then becomes one of drawing the plan first and then extruding up (or down) to the stair's landings. I urge my students to think of the stair much as they would if they were to build it: first lay it out, then build its landings and finally span each run of stair from landing to landing.

DRAWING SLOPES

A unique challenge for perspective observation

I have been blessed by spending much of my life living in Pittsburgh. It is a singular environment with steep hills overlooking rivers once lined by steel mills. Because our winters often have significant snowfalls, the roads here twist and turn along contours as they ascend and descend in order to maintain manageable rates of slope. As a result, they yield the constantly turning ascending and descending vistas that have been a focus of many of my murals.

I have also had the opportunity of working over a lengthy period in San Francisco. Owing to the less severe weather conditions there, the roads simply go straight up and down the slopes. And they are astonishingly steep; so steep that, as in the intersection to the right, viewers are apt to see the underside of a bus or car rising up out of a slope below!

Just the sheer three-dimensionality of these conditions—they engage all three spatial axes—makes drawing sloping roads a worthy subject. If you don't have such conditions nearby, photographs provide reasonable substitutes. Views of Italian hill towns or townscapes in the Greek islands will do just fine.

The key to drawing slopes is relating them initially to level conditions. Much as we did in drawing stairs, here we construct

2.88 Douglas Cooper with Grégoire Picher et al. *Medical Sciences Building Mural.*

2.87 Douglas Cooper with Grégoire Picher and assisted by Professor Judith Modell, Henry Weinberg, Jessica Bollinger, Melissa McMahon, Eric Lai. *Medical Sciences Building Mural.* University of California at San Francisco. 2002. Charcoal and acrylic on paper on board. 11' x 130'.

FREEHAND PERSPECTIVE 5
Views of hillside streets

Start by drawing a plan showing the foreground road segment (and houses). Then draw a perspective plan of the same condition. Draw a vertical at a convenient corner, draw a horizon line across it and refer to the original plan to align road segments to vanishing points along it.

If the road turns, draw tangents to these turning segments in the perspective plan. These tangents will still vanish along the horizon line, but their location will depend on the segment's alignment. Continue drawing the plan of the road segment by segment, then erect vanishing points above or below each segment's vanishing point— think stairs—and in this way draw the road above the perspective plan.

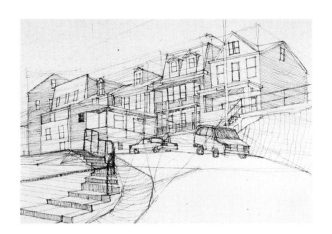

the streetscape first as if it were level, and then from that original datum, we raise the street up over that plan if it is ascending or depress it if it is descending. In each case, the key observations for vanishing points are the same ones we made when drawing stairs: namely, vanishing points for slopes are above or below the central vanishing point of their horizontal orientations. Put in a way that relates to everyday observation: the vanishing point for a sloping street will be above or below the vanishing point for the horizontal edges of a house paralleling that same street. The view above offers a clear instance of this. Note how the vanishing point for the slope is directly above the central vanishing point for the windows and roofline of the house on the corner.

Do not however consider this exercise to be one that is only about construction. Feeling the slope while you draw it—in the ways we have discussed in Chapter 1—

2.89 Opposite above: See on demonstration CD.
2.90 Opposite below: Charles Elliot.
2.91 Above left: Douglas Cooper. *Down Sterling Street*
(detail) 2006. Charcoal and acrylic on board.
2.92 Below: Jennifer Hanson.

should remain at the forefront. The drawing below right (Figure 2.92) is precise in its understanding of the underlying construction, but its forceful and supremely active linework allow the ascent and descent of the roadways to be felt at the same time.

When vistas turn

When vistas turn as they slope, a real opportunity arises, one that has become central to my own mural work in Pittsburgh. Seeing is, after all, a kinetic sense. We move while we see. We turn our heads. We look up; we look down. As an introduction to the next section on movement and perspective, and as in the vista above, it is good to try to capture the multiple directions of sight and turning vistas that a sloping roadway with a bend can activate.

MOVEMENT AND PERSPECTIVE

Gibson's later work: returning Gibson to Nicholaides

Without diminishing its value, Gibson's early work does make vision seem almost passive. Once we consider the world already ordered—pre-ordered we might say—vision seems reduced to a process of registering and recording: a role that seems at odds with daily experience. The progress of Gibson's later work recognizes this limitation. Beginning with *The Senses Considered as Perceptual Systems*, published sixteen years after *The Perception of the Visual World*, he gave much greater weight to the role of movement in visual perception. With his last work, *The Ecological Approach to Perception,* vision emerged as the much more dynamic sense of a perceiver who is constantly interacting with the environment.

Clearly then, movement is an issue for perspective. Perspective presents the view from a fixed position and looks in only one direction, yet we must acknowledge that we seldom view the world this way for long. We generally move while we look.

Others have already investigated this limitation of perspective. Cubist painters at the outset of the 20th century looked at the dynamic change of the visual image as a viewer moves. Reverse perspective (showing more than one aspect of the same object) is a constant of their work. More recently through painting and photography, David Hockney has systematically investigated ways in which vision changes as a viewer moves. As we conclude this section on Gibson's visual order and to return us to the more interactive sense of vision with which we started with Nicholaides, I present ways in which drawing—even perspective drawing—might acknowledge movement.

A Sculptor's Assignment

This issue has been central to my work since I was a student. My drawing teacher, Kent Bloomer, now at Yale, gave my class a strange assignment. In one drawing he asked us

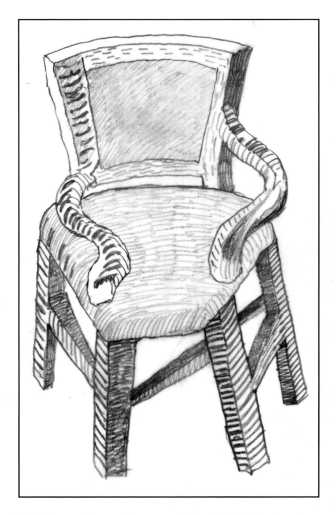

2.94 Reverse Perspective, recreation of David Hockney's *The Chair* (1985).

2.93 Opposite: Douglas Cooper with Jonathan Kline and John Trivelli. *Carnegie Mellon University Center Mural.* 1996. Charcoal and acrylic on board, 11' x 200'.

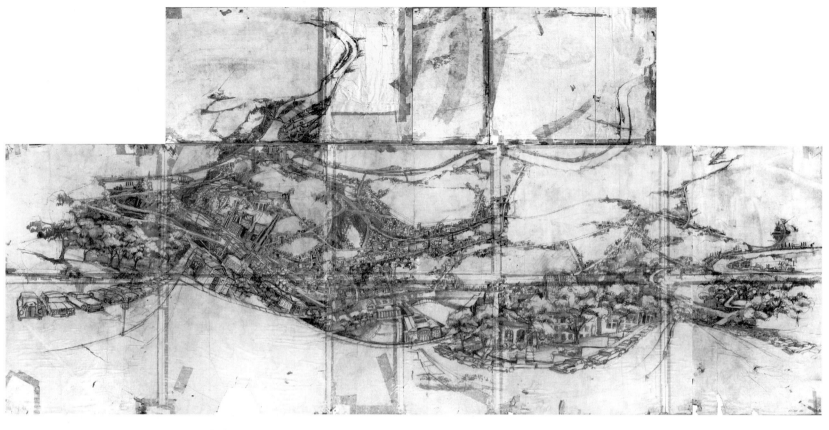

to draw everything inside our studio and everything outside as well. Kent is a sculptor, and the assignment had much to do with his trade. As a sculptor, he brought a natural skepticism about drawing to the class. Accustomed to considering his work in the full round and from all aspects, he distrusted the value of perspective for its limitation to one point of view. For models to pursue, Bloomer took us back before the reinvention of perspective: to proto-Renaissance painters such as Martini, Lorenzetti and Giotto. Their paintings often incorporated multiple standpoints and viewing directions, he said. And he described medieval images that showed interiors and exteriors in inventive

2.95 Above: Carnegie Mellon Campus. Drawing submitted in Kent Bloomer's class (1966).
2.96 Attributed to Giotto di Bondone (1266-1336). *The Saint Chases the Demons from Arezzo.* Alinari Art Resource.

cutaway views: perhaps showing a Duke conferring with his generals inside a castle and a battle raging outside.

Eventually his assignment led me outside to draw Pittsburgh landscapes where steep and twisting slopes presented the same multiple directions of view Bloomer had described earlier. They made me look upwards while I drew. They made me look downwards and turn and move along the street.

Taping drawings together

In the Pittsburgh landscape I also soon discovered a technique for showing more than one location in one drawing. It came by accident. I had nearly filled two adjacent sheets of bond paper with a wide-field drawing of the Carnegie Mellon campus, and I was wondering how I might also show some of the surrounding area. There was no room left, so I simply taped additional sheets around the original sheets. Seeing the campus drawing at the center of this new expanded context gave me an idea: why not view this new area from a different direction? And so the drawing proceeded as two drawings in one: the campus in the foreground viewed horizontally and the surrounding city in the background viewed from above.

Letting drawings out of the corner

Several years later, I resumed work on Bloomer's assignment during a sketching trip to Europe in 1969. While in London, I found that by taking the Circle Line I could visit most all of London's late-19th-century iron-and-glass covered train stations. What fascinated me about them was their breadth of field, which seemed to unfold endlessly in every direction.

At first working in the small format of my travel sketchbook seemed difficult. But eventually at Paddington Station I found an obvious solution: drawing small in one corner. I was on a walkway overlooking the tracks. I began by looking down the length of the train shed and drawing a small and fairly static perspective at the top left corner. After letting it reach some conclusion, I then let the drawing expand more impulsively.

As the drawing blossomed from the corner, the edge of the page began to exert an unavoidable force. Unlike the taped together drawings in Pittsburgh,

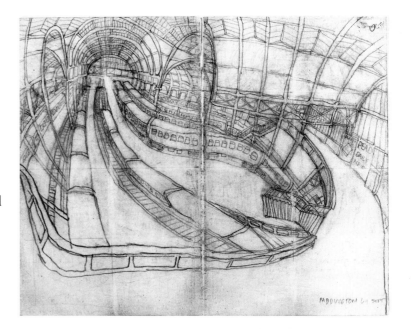

2.97 Above top right: Douglas Cooper. *Paddington Station*. 1969. Graphite on paper. 8"x10".
2.98 Above lower right: Douglas Cooper. *Trajan's Market*. 1969. Graphite on paper, 8"x10".

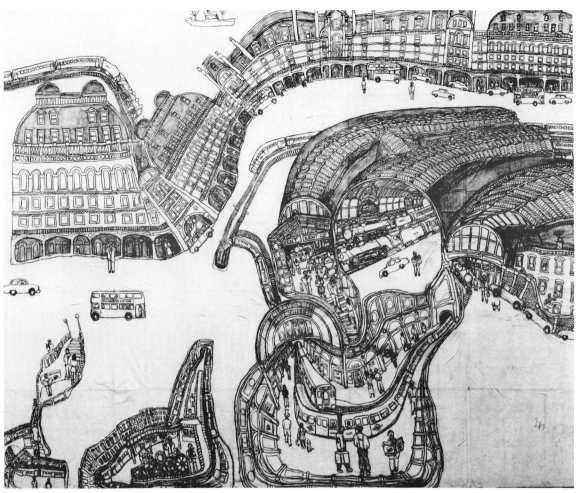

2.99 Douglas Cooper. *From Paddington to Victoria.*
1970. Charcoal on paper, 6' x 8'. Carnegie Museum,
Pittsburgh, PA.

which always had the option of further expansion, my sketchbook had a boundary I could not exceed. Whatever I had initiated by letting the drawing out of the corner, I had to complete by the edge of the page. The drawing became a race for available space: turning, squeezing and distorting things in order to fit them in before the drawing reached the edge.

Time and memory

Other drawings took interesting turns because of time pressure. On our last day in Rome, my wife Meg and I had arrived late at Trajan's Market. The guard was tired and determined to leave by closing time, fifteen minutes away. A small bribe secured us half an hour. Walking in, I asked Meg to go one way while I went another. Meg went up and down every stair and along every arcade. Meanwhile, I drew. I began in the upper-left-hand corner of my sketchbook with an image of the main upper market hall. We met half an hour later at the gate, and then, while I continued drawing, Meg described the things she had seen, and I fit these into what I had begun.

The scenario of this drawing in the market—half life-drawing, half memory-drawing—fascinated me. So it was this kind of drawing that I resumed when I returned to Pittsburgh. In one image I wanted to string together the many sketches I had done at the London stations in order to reconstruct a memory of my trips on the Circle Line.

It was by then early October 1969 and I began the drawing as the New York Mets in the culmination of their "miracle season" opened the World Series with the Baltimore Orioles. I drew as I listened on the radio. I drew from sketches. I drew from memory. Starting in the middle with a sketch I had done on site at Paddington, I pieced the drawing together: picture by picture, memory by memory. Rarely does a drawing proceed with an energy all its own as this one did. Just like the Mets that October, or so it seemed, this drawing was an irresistible force. I just tried to stay out of the way and let it happen!

Drawing Pittsburgh

I have drawn Pittsburgh for many of the years since that assignment, and its aftermath. Kent Bloomer's assignment has meant a career for me. In more recent years, the work has become more recognizable in imagery than those early works based on my European trip, but it has continued to build on the basic moves of those years: 1) expanded breadth of field, 2) looking up and down, 3) moving locations while drawing, 4) letting vanishing points slide a bit, 5) showing what's out of sight, and maybe only remembered. These central moves are the ones with which you might begin.

2.100 Douglas Cooper. *St. Johns and McCardle Roadway.* Charcoal and acrylic on paper on board. 1998. 48" x 96". (Private collection).

DRAWING COMPLEXITY

The limits of analysis

Reining ourselves in once again after our brief exploration of vision as a kinetic sense, let's return for the moment to the geometry of the objects we draw. Until now most of our subjects have been readily adapted to perspective. We have drawn buildings with architectural features such as cornices and regular column intervals. Even more difficult subjects such as stairs and slopes have seemed to possess inherent and accessible information that we could use to understand their order and eventually draw them. But what shall we do with conditions where geometric order is not readily apparent? How, for example, shall we draw the conditions of an undulating landscape, or a cliff-face or a piece of fruit? Even considering man-made objects, where geometry might be expected to be more apparent, how might we draw the rounded shapes of a 1950s-era car, an airplane or the hull of a boat?

2.101 How shall we draw the conditions of an undulating landscape or a cliff face or a piece of fruit? Anne Riggs.

FREEHAND PERSPECTIVE 6
Views of curvilinear objects

When drawing a car or an airplane or even a horse, start by imposing a set of sectional cuts upon the subject. Draw these planes in perspective and use them to impart order to the subject.

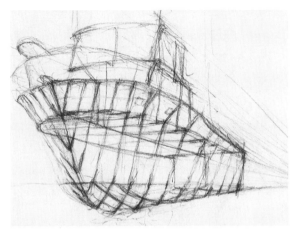

2.102 Kyle Gardner.

2.103 Ju-Kay Kwek.

2.104 Toy airplane.

Drawing rounded forms

The key to drawing rounded forms is thinking of their sectional characteristics. We cut sections through them, and we use these to generate their appearance. Some of you may have at some point made a toy model airplane such as the one pictured at left. In effect, the toy abstracts the complex curved forms of the fuselage and wings into a set of sectional cuts, and a correct representation of these shapes results from the correct alignment of these sections. Such is our approach to drawing the 1950s-era Studebaker and boat hulls shown above. We start with sections, in these cases with sections in multiple directions, and proceed from them.

GOING BEYOND THE INFORMATION GIVEN

In fact, the highly geometric process we just used in drawing curved objects was not all that unrelated to the nature of the objects themselves. Airplanes, cars and boats are often manufactured quite like the way they are modeled in the toy at lower left—and the way we just went about drawing them. Airplane wings are made with aligned struts, fuselages and car bodies with ring-like sections and boat hulls with ribs. But there was also a hint of the artificial in the process we just used—one that we should also note. We started by imposing something on the thing we were about to draw—sectional cuts—and then we used those to draw the object.

Let me illustrate the artificiality of such impositions with this example. Consider the problems that might arise for us if we were drawing a horse. In order to understand the animal and place it in space, we might very well begin by imposing a set of sectional cuts on it as well. Although horses do have ribs to be sure, the sectional cuts we would impose on our horse would only marginally relate to their physical facts and to this extent the order we would be using would have originated with us. This kind of drawing built on imposed order will become the focus of Chapter 3.

When we began this volume with Nicholaides, how we made marks, how we related mark making to the sense of touch, and how we moved while drawing all became key subjects for our drawing. Our interaction with our subjects was the initiator of the process. In Chapter 2 with Gibson, we have focused upon the order present in our subjects. At times, almost passively, we have relied upon our subjects to deliver the order, which would guide us through the process. Now as we move to Chapter 3, we will consider what you the artist might bring to the process. I am not speaking here of expression, but conception. Initially with imposed geometric constructions and thereafter with proactive reads of light, shadow and color, we will investigate how the sense of order you might bring to bear on the process might structure the act of drawing.

When Order is Made

WHEN ORDER IS MADE

A Trip to Bryce Canyon

The sense that I might be more proactive with what I was drawing came to me all at once while I was on a sketching trip. I was drawing some rock formations in Bryce Canyon in Southern Utah, and I found that I simply could not grasp the three-dimensionality of what I was drawing without first injecting something of myself into the work.

I was not the first to have been so inspired by Bryce, for the canyon is a unique place. Filled with immense eroded spires, it exists at a potent level of abstraction. People have described it as an immense dribble-castle spread over a 50 square-mile area. It is a playground for what psychologists call "projective imagery," that very interesting process of attaching meaning to something while perceiving it in error. A simple example would be looking out an airplane window and seeing the face of Abe Lincoln in a cloud formation.[1] In Bryce Canyon people look at rock formations and see all sorts of things. Some see people—one spire is named Queen Victoria. I tend to see architectural imagery such as castles and gothic churches. Others see beasts and animals. The canyon is a bigger than life-size "Rorsach Test" in stone.

Order originates with the viewer

Given my predicament while drawing in Bryce, the interesting thing about projective imagery is the direction of the assignment of meaning. Meaning originates with the viewer and is directed at what is seen. This is different from what we grew accustomed to in the previous chapter. There with Gibson's help, we considered order to be something

---

[1] Projective imagery was first studied in depth by Gestalt psychologists. Because preexisting schemata form a central perceptual mechanism for them, in a loose way this chapter does align with Gestalt psychology. Order is considered as originating with the viewer. However, the parallel should not be taken too far. There is no argument here that perspective is a schema with which viewers are born.

3.0 Overleaf: When order is made. Photo: Mirko Krizanovic.
3.1 Opposite: A playland for projective imagery: Bryce Canyon Utah.

3.2 Imposing perspective on a scene in Bryce Canyon,
Utah. Pen on paper, 11"x 14" (1990).

arising in the world around us: something we needed only to register. As it concerns
perspective, we keyed on linear details such as cornices and column intervals, and thus
were able to see, read, and recreate the perspective order implicit in whatever building we
were drawing. Though at times we imposed some geometric constructions on our work,
these only had the purpose of clarifying order that we believed to be there already. But
with the example of Bryce Canyon, we see evidence that order can also originate with the
beholder.

In Bryce I was finding I had to do more than just observe. There were some formal
clues in the stonework already to be sure. The stone in Bryce is sedimentary. It's
limestone with various amounts of iron, and owing to varying rates of erosion it has very
pronounced horizontal lines. But these clues were insufficient to understand the three-

dimensional order of what I was drawing. Instead I had to use sectional constructions, like the ones shown at left, along cardinal orientations in order to fully grasp shapes. It was easier when I forced these networks onto the formations and used them as a filter to understand the natural conditions beyond my grasp.

It occurs to me that what I was doing that summer with these sketches very much parallels the mechanism of projective imagery I described above. Yes, I was responding to what I was drawing. But the order I was using, the x,y,z coordinate system, was mine. It originated with me, not the rocks I was drawing. Perhaps we use perspective in this way more often than we think, not just with rocks in a place as strange as Bryce Canyon, but even with buildings where perspective seems obvious.

Perspective: a chicken and egg issue

In the previous chapter, I had hinted that perspective might be more than just an observable fact of the environment, and I had suggested that there is something of a "chicken and egg" issue that surrounds the subject. Does perspective exist as observable perceptual law for all to see, or does the world only seem to appear in perspective after we first understand the concept?

There is an interesting parallel to this issue—perspective as observable fact vs. perspective as imposed construct—in the history of its development during the early Renaissance. Like myself in Bryce Canyon, early Renaissance painters also ran into a problem they simply could not solve through observation alone.

Alberti and the problem of the diagonal

With our perspective constructions in earlier chapters, we have guessed at increments of foreshortening. In fact this is exactly what early Renaissance painters did until Leon Battista Alberti (1404–1472) codified a method called the *construzione leggitima.* In views with single vanishing points, artists had already known how to make lines recede to common points. They had used a system called *"Pavimenti,"* meaning floor tiles, and had laid out pictures as grid-works on the floor of the view at the start. They had simply measured equal increments along the view's base, and had converged lines through these intervals to a common vanishing point.

But they had been left with guesswork to determine the projected depths of the tiles as they receded into the scene. Various methods had been used, some based on observation and some on arithmetic systems. A popular standard had been to reduce successive intervals by a third. But the problem with all these methods was that none had resulted in straight diagonals—something that troubled a person of Alberti's mathematical precision.

Alberti supplanted his contemporaries' empirical methods in *Della Pittura* (1435),

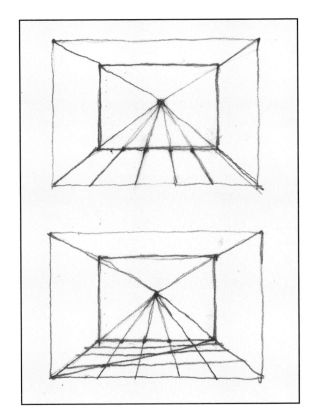

3.3 Early Renaissance painters knew how to project longitudinal lines to common vanishing points, but until they learned to use a diagonal, they could not accurately foreshorten units of depth.

PROJECTING PERSPECTIVE 1
Free-hand magic method

ON THE CD

Draw the geometry of the end wall as the view's picture plane. Locate the horizon line, central vanishing point, and convergent lines out from it. On the horizon line, find the vanishing point for a 45°. This must be the same distance to the right or left of the center of vision as you are from the end wall. On that side, develop a ruler (same scale as the end wall) of key increments of depth. Start it from the lower corner of the end wall and extend it outward along the wall's base line. From the vanishing point for the 45° angle, draw lines through points on your scale to corresponding points of intersection with the side of the floor of your space. These points represent correctly foreshortened increments of depth. Use them to generate the geometry of the space.

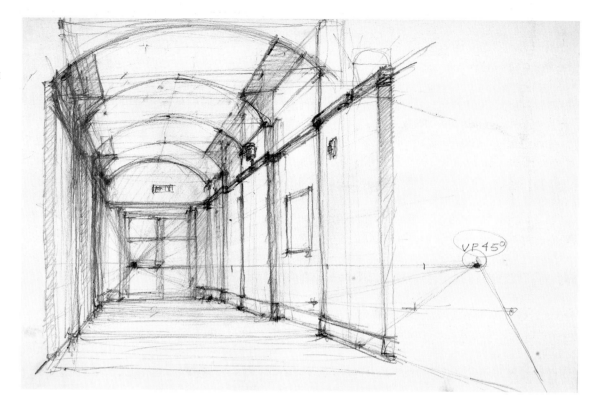

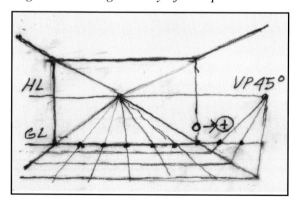

3.4 Above right: See on demonstration CD.
3.5 The magic method projected forward from the picture plane.

the first codification of perspective, and the diagonal was the key.[2] Alberti understood the general rule for finding vanishing points—for a given line, they are found by drawing a line parallel to that line from the viewer's position to a point of intersection on the picture plane. What Alberti observed was a special case. In a one-point view with the picture plane set at the back wall of a space, the vanishing point for a 45° angle must be the same distance to the left or right of the viewer's center of vision as that viewer is located from the end wall picture plane (this being the case because 45° triangles have two equal sides). The utility of finding the vanishing point for a 45° line was compelling. In a one-point view, a diagonal drawn across a set of equidistant convergent lines must, in crossing that set, generate correct intervals in depth. Alberti's discovery, today called the "magic method," and shown above, was one of the major advances of the Renaissance.

---

[2] Alberti's method of one-point perspective entered common practice. This method, today called the "magic method," can be used for quick free-hand views. It is discussed in detail in the Appendix.

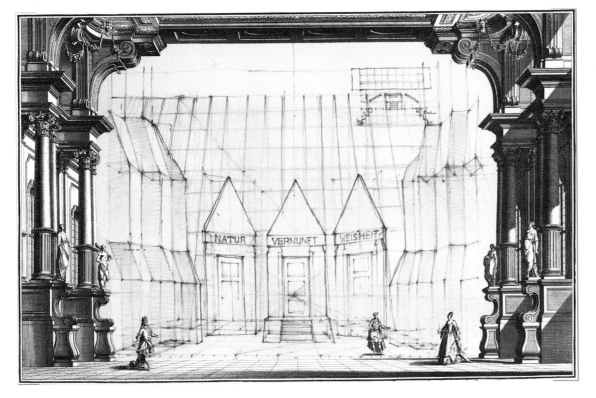

Draw the proscenium large enough to serve as the view's picture plane. Over it locate the horizon line, a central vanishing point opposite someone in an imagined audience, and convergent lines out from it. Along the horizon line locate the vanishing point for a 45°angle. On that side, develop a ruler of key increments of depth. Start it from the lower corner of the proscenium and extend it along the inside of the proscenium's base line. From the vanishing point for the 45° angle, draw lines through points on the scale to corresponding points of intersection with the side of the floor of the stage space back of the proscenium. These points represent correctly foreshortened increments of depth.

The magic method and stage set design

The magic method is extremely useful in stage set design. Assuming a proscenium theater, there are two basic approaches: setting the picture plane at the back of the stage and measuring locations forward—what we used above left—or setting the picture plane at the position of the proscenium and working backward—what is shown above.

Measuring back of the picture plane is similar to measuring forward. The only difference is where the ruler is set. Whereas before we set the ruler to the outside of the picture plane, here we set the ruler to the inside of the picture plane and then measure back with diagonals (using the vanishing point for the 45° angle) to the backward projection of the side of the space.

Using diagonals in two-point views.

A variant of Alberti's system is useful for two-point views as well. What is required is a quick but well-proportioned plan. In that plan insert a picture plane: perpendicular to your viewing angle. After finding the two spatial vanishing points along that picture

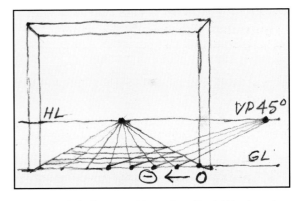

3.6 Above left: Stage set based on David Hockney's design for *The Magic Flute*, foreground from Giuseppe Galli Bibiena, from Architectural and Perspective Designs, Dover Publications Inc. New York: 1964.
3.7 The magic method behind the picture plane.

PROJECTING PERSPECTIVE 3
Two-point views using diagonals

Start by drawing a small plan of your space. In it indicate your position, a viewing angle, a picture plane, vanishing points for x and y axes, and the vanishing point for a 45°angle.

As in earlier two-point views, draw a major corner of the space with a vertical line and position the horizon line across this vertical. Then along the horizon line, locate vanishing points for the two spatial axes and one of the vertical edges of the end wall.

From the corner of the end wall, generate the geometry of the end wall. Proportion one bay, then use method of doubling intervals to generate other bays.

Use your plan to estimate the position of a vanishing point for a 45°angle. Think of its location in bay increments. For example in the plan of the example above, the vanishing point of a 45°angle is ca. two bay widths from the interior corner of the double-height space. Use this to locate the vanishing point, of the 45°angle along the horizon line.

Use the vanishing point for the 45°angle to generate accurately foreshortened lateral intervals across the space.

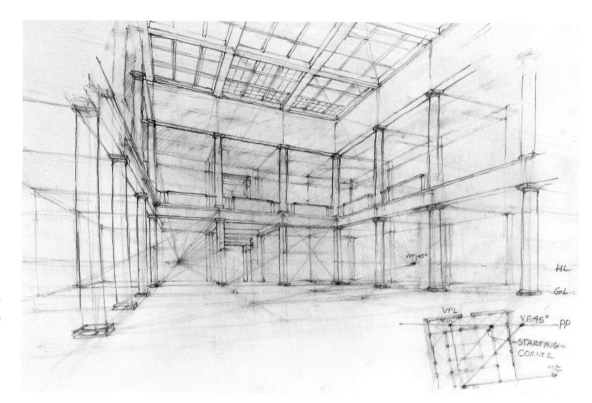

3.8 Perspective using diagonals.

plane, generate a vanishing point for a spatial diagonal. Generate it first in plan. Then use that construction to approximate its location along the horizon line. Finally use a spatial diagonal to generate a grid-work of equally spaced increments forward.

Alberti and the invention of the station point

In fact Alberti went further than just solving the problem of the diagonal. He presented a general understanding of the underlying optics of perspective based on the view from an individual observer. To model perspective he proposed something he called the "visual pyramid." Points on objects were projected through a picture plane to the viewer, thereby generating an image that bore a measurable relationship to the object in the picture.[3] His construction served to unify for the first time the relationship between the objects in a scene, the picture plane, and the viewer.

---

[3] White, John. *The Birth and Rebirth of Pictorial Space* (Boston: Boston Book and Art Shop, 1967) pp.121–126.

Alberti's stance was much more interventionist than his contemporaries. Not content, as they were, to base his understanding on observation alone, he imposed a unified construction upon the world first, and it was through the lens of that order, so to speak, that he observed objects in the world.

What does this mean for us? In our approach to perspective until this chapter, we, like Alberti's contemporaries, have used observation alone. But Alberti's work suggests that we no longer think of objects in isolation—the images of the individual buildings seen from individual directions in the *Bigallo Fresco* discussed in the previous chapter come to mind. Instead, we must consider (and draw) objects as part of a larger spatial conception. We have to think of a continuous perspective space first and then place objects in it—rather than the other way around.

This idea is not entirely new with Alberti. Consider foreshortening. Consider the horses in the mosaic the *Battle at Issus* (discussed in the last chapter) and what spatial conception might have led to their being so accurately foreshortened. It was one that from the outset required the original Greek painter to consider the horses as parts of the larger order of the whole picture: as participants in the ongoing battle arrayed on the field. Understood in that larger context, the horses had to occupy space and hold spatial relationships relative to the other combatants. It was as participants in that greater whole that they were foreshortened, not as individual horses.

On the wings of Uccello

With respect to my experience in Bryce Canyon and in light of Alberti's work in perspective, one of the most interesting early perspective painters was Paolo Uccello (1397–1475). Uccello loved perspective, indeed so much so that he was severely criticized by his contemporaries for being obsessed with it. To my eye his most interesting works are those where he seems to get some things in true perspective and some things not. His image of the *Rout at San Romagna* (ca. 1450: See Figure 3.12) is a mural-sized image in several panels whose background landscape seems almost a throwback to earlier proto-Renaissance painters. Its interesting shifts in scale and somewhat upturned surface present a wonderful foil for the foreground. With that foreground, in particular its ground surface, Uccello is fully in tune with the latest perspective tricks of his day, and he takes perspective even further than his contemporaries.

3.9 Depiction of Alberti's understanding of the picture plane. Albrecht Dürer (1471–1528), Artist drawing a Model in Foreshortening through a plane using a grid system. Woodcut from *Unterweysung der Messung* (Treatise on Perspective). (Nuremburg, 1527. B.149). Photo: Marburg/Art Resource, NY.
3.10 *Battle of Issus*. (detail). Mosaic. Museo Archeologico Nazionale, Naples, Italy. Alinari/Art Resource, NY.

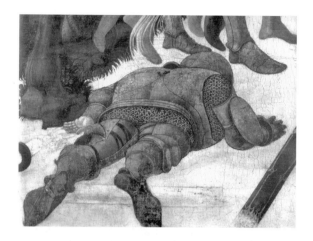

3.11-3.12 Paolo Uccello. (1397–1475). *The Rout of San Romano* (and detail) ca. 1450, National Gallery, London.
3.13-3.14 Opposite below and above: Paolo Uccello. (1397-1475). Perspective Studies of a Mazzocchio and a chalice (latter modified for clarity). Uffizi, Florence, Italy. Alinari/Art Resource, NY.
3.15 Opposite below right: Map of Europe using Ben Sylvester's method.

Not content to merely report the events of the battle in perspective, he intervened with perspective into the event itself. The poor fellows who perish in his battle do not merely die. They die in perfect one-point perspective convergence! And dutifully for Uccello's purposes, they apparently have the good sense in their last moments of life to cast down their weapons as well—once again in perfect one-point convergence.[4]

Uccello is credited by some—Piero della Francesca (1420?–1492) is another—as being one of the first to move beyond Alberti's grid system to a scheme of projecting perspectives from plans and elevations, the procedure that is presented in conventional form in the Appendix of this book. What is certain is that over the course of his life, Uccello developed an extraordinary facility for understanding odd-shaped objects in perspective, even objects that are not immediately recognizable for their perspective content at all. Two of his most remarkable drawings show a chalice and a *mazzocchio,* a hollow ring of wickerwork used for a Renaissance headdress. Looking at these objects with their globe-like portrayal, we are immediately struck by Uccello's understanding of

---

[4] Wright, Lawrence. *Perspective on Perspective* (London, Boston, Melbourne and Henley: Routledge & Kegan Paul, 1983) pp. 70–79.

the order that would underlie Mercator's (1512–1594) maps, one century later, with their lines of longitude and latitude.

An analogy to maps

Whether there is a link between perspective's reemergence in the early Renaissance and Mercator's subsequent maps may be open to speculation, but it does make sense to compare the process of map making—which portrays irregular land shapes—and the process of drawing irregular shapes in perspective. Both project an x,y coordinate system out into the world and use that system to order what is represented.

Years ago at the Choate School in Wallingford, CT, I had a geography teacher named Ben Sylvester who so loved his subject that he taught us to draw maps of all the world's continents—from memory. We had to include all nations, geographic features, and major cities. He showed us his own personal system, which used squares with named locations at each corner. We then simply laid out the squares and, based on them, we could correctly proportion and locate land masses, rivers, countries etc. When we drew Europe, for example, we started with Prague. One square north of it was Stettin. One square west was Frankfurt. And so we proceeded: laying out the locator points first and then building the map over top.

A similar process can be used for perspectives with irregular conditions. We need only construct a plan of the space we wish to draw and lay a grid over top of it. Then in perspective, we reverse the process. First we construct a perspective grid. Then we construct the irregular plan within that grid and build the drawing of the space up from it.

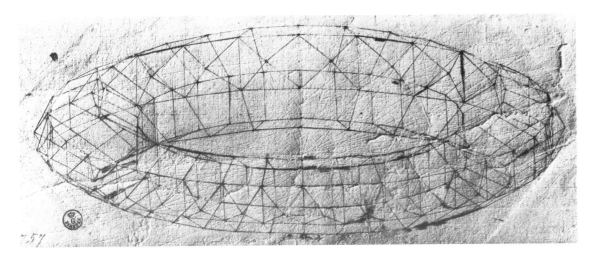

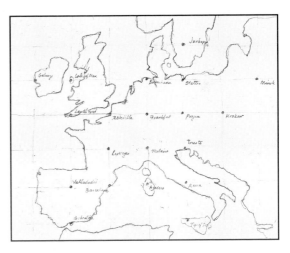

PROJECTING PERSPECTIVE 4
Mapping multi-point views

ON
THE
CD

Find a space like the oval space shown at right. Then much as you have done in Exercise 3, draw its plan and then, starting at any convenient point, construct a plan grid over top.

Begin the perspective by drawing this plan grid in perspective, and then map the irregular space into your plan grid. Where curves are bounded by faceted planes, as in the example at right, develop these planes first as cords in plan, then extend these cords to vanishing points and then use each of three vanishing points respectively to generate each facet.

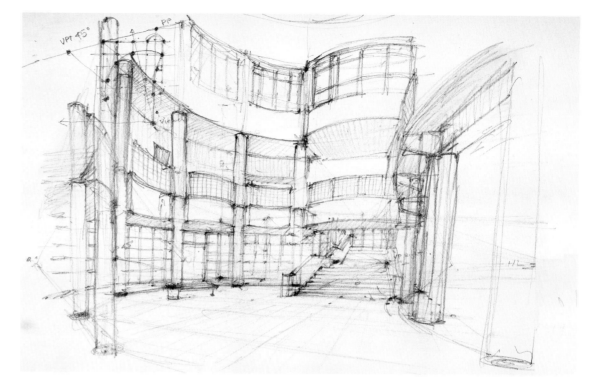

3.16 Above right: See on demonstration CD.
3.17 Above: A train rounding a bend shows the vanishing points of cords. Base painting from: Grif Teller. Pennsylvania Railroad Calendar 1953.

Extracting vanishing points
This method of generating irregular plan shapes in perspective allows us to draw complex wall orientations like those in the oval space above. We do this by a process of extracting vanishing points from a perspective plan. We let the picture itself develop them. To understand how this process works, first consider a railroad train rounding a bend and the perspective relationships its individual cars embody. Each car is at a different angle, and therefore each must have its own vanishing point. But their vanishing points do share something in common. Because the cars are all level to the ground, their vanishing points must all lie on the horizon line. And this fact—a set of turning segmented planes with vanishing points all on the horizon line—helps us draw curving planes.

First we define the curving plan shape as a set of cords—think railroad cars on a bend. We simply draw these cords in the projected perspective plan—by plotting each cord in the projected plan—and then we extend each cord to a point of intersection with the horizon line. The vanishing points thus found serve as the vanishing points for the plane facets, which border the curved space.

The pose should foreshorten the front or side. Draw the pose as a set of planes. Identify cardinal planes in the pose—front, side etc. Then visualize where corners might exist between these planes (reclined and twisted poses are good). Consider each plane to have a singular spatial orientation and related convergence. Exaggerate that convergence by extending convergent lines beyond the figure's boundary. In the spirit of Uccello, don't just draw what is visible; use sectional cuts to draw what is out of sight.

Imposing perspective: using sections on landscape

What we began with Alberti's sense of continuous perspective order, we will now pursue with Uccello's sense of imposed order. As we draw the figure above and then landscapes on the following pages, we will force perspective into them. Yes, we will respond to what is already present in each condition, but in the end we will impose perspective order onto all things we draw, whatever their nature, be they houses hills, or kumquats.

Beyond their relationship to map making, Uccello's chalice and *mazzocchio* (Figures 3.13, 3.14) used a technique that becomes important as we now begin using perspective to draw landscapes: namely his transparent use of sectional cuts. The drawing of the *mazzocchio* used 32 hexagons rotated through the form. The chalice shows horizontal contours that go completely around it and allow us to see its backside. For Uccello, not only was space continuous, but surface as well. And he used rotated sections to get from one to the other: ordering the backside with the same understanding as the front.

As we use Uccello's sectional cuts in the landscape, we are building on the last exercise from Chapter 2: *Views of curvilinear objects* (page 142)—but with two important differences.

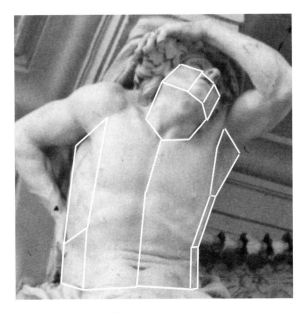

3.18 Above left: Yella Lee.
3.19 Above middle: Xianghua Wu.
3.20 Imposing cardinal orientations on the figure.

PROJECTING PERSPECTIVE 6
Imposing perspective on landscapes

Find an interesting sloping scene with few houses and much exposed ground. Use a horizon line to construct a plan grid extending back in space. This plane will serve as a reference plane or "datum" for your work. Locate roads and buildings as projected plane shapes. Build sloping roadways and ground surfaces up or down from this plane, using sectional cuts to generate each in perspective. Over several drawings, gradually increase the level of difficulty, by drawing progressively more rural scenes.

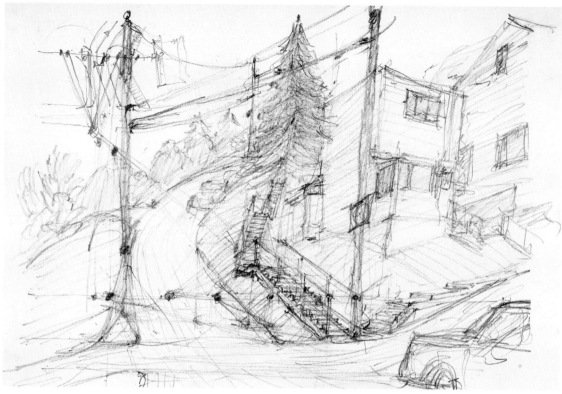

3.21 Above right: See on demonstration CD.
3.22 Imposing perspective on sloping ground.

There we used sectional cuts in all three cardinal orientations. Here, as a way of visualizing the surface of the ground, we need to make explicit reference of these sectional cuts to a plan drawn in perspective, and we also need to use some of the observations of slopes, which we made when drawing sloping streets (Chapter 2, page 132).

Few settings for the landscape exercise at right are better than golf courses. They offer an ideal mix of the natural and the artificial. Their ubiquitous cart paths present directional and sectional information. Mowing patterns on fairways tend to follow parallel contours. But another characteristic of golf courses also points us toward the history of perspective post-Uccello, which we shall consider shortly. Golf courses present perspective illusions designed to trick players into misjudging the distance of their shots. With perspective illusions we often even misjudge what we are seeing.

Grand illusions: perspective after Uccello

Uccello's *Rout at San Romano,* with its extraordinary depiction of fallen soldiers in perspective convergence, marked a turning point in the use of perspective. In this

3.23 Above left: Esther I. Chen.
3.24 Unknown artist.
3.25 Imposing sectional cuts on a golf course.

remarkable painting, the order of perspective is not just one that is implicit in the environment, as it was for Gibson. Nor is it one that might be used to impart order to the visual world as it was for Alberti. After Uccello, perspective could become order unto itself. At the heart of this was the Mannerist and Baroque use of perspective illusion.

To work, perspective illusions must presume knowledge of perspective on the part of viewers. Like jokes whose punch lines presume contextual knowledge, perspective illusions only work if viewers already know perspective. They need to project perspective order out into the scene in order to see it in error.

San Ignazio and other illusions

I well remember the first time I saw a perspective illusion. Before my first trip to Rome, a friend had urged me to go see San Ignazio. "You'll be surprised!" he said. Several weeks later I entered the central doorway at San Ignazio. Having visited several Baroque churches already—I had just come from Il Gesu—I saw what I had grown accustomed to

seeing at other churches in Rome: a long barrel-vaulted nave and a cupola at the crossing. Then I moved several paces to the right, and the cupola appeared to fall over.

In fact there was no cupola. In its place was a fairly flat disk painted to look like a cupola from my viewing position near the entrance. Moving further into the church, I looked up and saw the ceiling fresco, which runs the length of the nave and which was even more impressive than the cupola. It depicted St. Ignatius' ascent into Heaven—with the architecture of the church and a host of angels all accompanying him up through the cloudscape of the sky. The fresco is so well executed that, as I gazed up at it, I could not accurately tell where the real architecture left off and the illusion began.

The family that executed these marvelous frescos at San Ignazio was named Pozzo. As I grew more familiar with their work both at San Ignazio and other sites, I learned how they had realized their fantastic illusions. For our understanding of the proactive stance of this chapter, the fresco over the nave is instructive.

Their task was not easy: how to construct a perspective image on the curved inside of the nave's barrel vault. They accomplished it step-by-step. First they drew a small cartoon of the final image they wanted viewers to see and imposed a grid over it. Then from the cornice of the barrel-vault's two sidewalls, they strung a grid work across the nave, equivalent to the one drawn over their cartoon. Then they located a point in the middle of the floor of the nave (if you visit San Ignazio, you will still find a brass disk at this point). This point would serve as their view's station point. From this point they strung taught wires up through the grid work, and up to the surface of the vault. With these sightlines, they were then able to map their cartoon image onto the vault.

What is key here is the direction of their image-making process. It originated at the station point—with the viewer, not with what is viewed—and from there, much like a slide in a slide projector, it was projected up onto the surface of the vault above. [5]

3.26 When I moved to the right, the cupola appeared to fall over. Andrea Pozzo (1642–1709). *Cupola in Perspective*. S. Ignazio, Rome, Italy. Photo: Scala/Art Resource.

3.27 I could not tell where the real architecture left off and the illusion began. Andrea Pozzo (1642–1709). *The Glorification of St. Ignatius*, ceiling fresco 1691–1699. S. Ignazio, Rome, Italy. Photo: Scala/Art Resource.

This kind of illusion, in which image orders and alters reality, had already been used in the century preceding San Ignazio. It was first seen in the stage-craft illusions of Andrea Palladio's *Teatro Olimpico*. This fixed stage piece provides a circumstance of street vistas that effectively enlarge the perceived depth of the stage, making it appear deeper than it truly is. We find similar uses in Bernini's *Sala Reggia* at the Vatican.

Gibson's textural gradient is helpful in understanding why these work. The two side surfaces of these vistas are in fact not parallel to one another. They are *raked* or turned slightly inward, not so much as to be obviously out of parallel, but just enough to offer viewers too much surface, without their realizing it. Gibson might describe the condition in this way. Effectively each provides a textural gradient commensurate with a much deeper longitudinal surface, and that deeper surface, supplanting the condition that is truly there, is what the viewer perceives instead.

---

[5] Wright, Lawrence. *Perspective on Perspective* (London, Boston, Melbourne and Henley: Routledge & Kegan Paul, 1983) pp. 143–144.

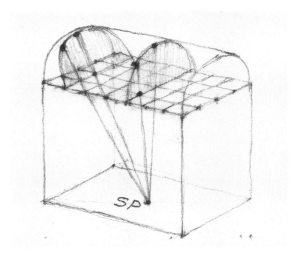

3.28 The perspective order originates with the viewer. Projecting the image at S. Ignazio.

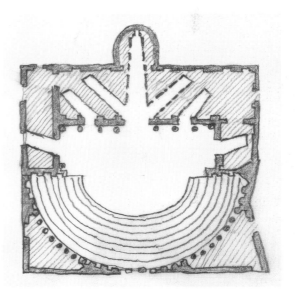

3.29 Above: Plan of the *Teatro Olimpico*.
3.30 Left: Andrea Palladio (1508–1580). Interior of the *Teatro Olimpico* 1589, *Teatro Olimpico*, Vicenza, Italy. Photo: Eric Lessing/ Art Resource, NY.

LIGHT AND DARK (AND COLOR)

Study of relationships, not absolutes

We have already addressed one depth cue, *linear perspective,* in the proactive spirit of this chapter. Now we will turn to another, *shade and shadow,* and treat it in that same way. Rather than just reading order from the environment around us, we will force our own order onto what we draw. Our work with *shade and shadow* and more generally with light and dark will lead us ultimately to color.

The study of light and dark and color is a study of relationships, not absolutes. Daily life offers frequent relational perceptions. Something may appear "tall" to us, but this perception always implies a relationship to something else. I am six feet tall. That is an absolute measure of sorts. But it is not a perceptual one. My perceived height can vary in accordance with my context. I will look tall and lanky next to jockey Eddie Arcaro and undeniably short next to basketball player Wilt Chamberlain.

Such is the case with many properties of light and dark and color. In absolute terms a fully saturated [6] red is a middle dark color. In a continuum of fully saturated swatches of yellow, orange, green, blue and violet, red would rank about in the middle in value: [7] lighter than blue and violet, slightly darker than green, much darker than yellow and orange.

Yet despite this absolute measure of the value of red, we can perceive the same red as either dark or light depending upon its context. Placed next to the warm black background of the cola in the bottle at right, the familiar *Coca-Cola* red will appear positively luminous. But in the context of the white graphic on the bottle's label or

3.32 Coca-Cola red is both lighter than the soft drink and darker than the graphic.

---

[6] Saturation: the amount of a particular hue in a color.
[7] Value: measure of its lightness or darkness.

3.31 Opposite: Douglas Cooper. *Past Summers.* 1997. Charcoal and acrylic on paper on bd, 48" x 96".

on the carton, that very same red will look dark. Did the darkness of the color change between the one circumstance and the other? No, what did change was the context and with it our perception. Such relational judgements will be at the heart of our approach to light and dark and color drawing.

Sharpen and emphasize contrasts

In looking at light and color, it is important to search out, sharpen, and even exaggerate contrasts. Contrast is a matter of both composition and conception, and it can be used to underscore both depth and content. Some of my favorite drawings of light and dark that do this are by German illustrator Hans Hillmann, who presented a beautifully illustrated version of Dashiell Hammett's *Fly Paper,* a gangster story set in San Francisco.[8]

Throughout his book, Hillmann artfully exploits the contrast of juxtaposed areas of light and dark. Like a *film noir* director, he arranges and choreographs his scenes as layers of overlapping light and dark profiles with great cinematic effect. The two scenes at the right, the "before" and "during" of a barroom brawl, have many adjacencies of light and dark that underscore the stiff tension of the moment before the fray and the chaos that ensues. In the first scene, the bald bartender apprehensively stands out along with the labels of his liquor bottles: white against the dark bar. The waitress furtively stands between the potential adversaries, her hair dark against the light bar, her white arm rigid against its base and her legs a stiff dark against the bright floor. The white of the table and bar in combination present a tense zig-zag space that suggests that something has to "give."

What gives is a "donnybrook" of dark against white, white against black, with arms and legs and torsos every which way.

As we proceed, we will also discover that light and shadow offer important information about the surfaces and shapes of objects. As we noted in the previous chapter's discussion of depth cues, light casts shadows on objects and models their forms in shade. The contours of these shadows and shades reveal the forms of the objects on which they are cast. We will start with this observation, and we will start with a highly simplified approach.

---

[8] Fliegenpapier is the German translation of Dashiell Hammett's *Fly Paper*, illustrated by Hans Hillmann (Frankfurt am Main: Zweitausendeins, 1982) pp. 22,34.

3.33-3.34 Opposite: Hans Hillmann. Illustrations from Fliegenpapier (Courtesy: Frau Hillmann).

LIGHT AND DARK 1
Imposing Two Values on the Figure
<u>*Ink, 1/4" brush, bond paper*</u>

The pose should be under harsh light that emphasizes shade and shadow. Represent the surface of the model as either dark (black ink) or light (blank page). Squinting helps this proactive simplification. Start from the centers of darker areas (avoid outlining) and then gradually enlarge them. Simultaneously consider both their shapes and those of the adjacent white areas.

3.35 Unknown artist.
3.36 Below left: Anne Riggs.

From simplicity to complexity
In working with value (light and dark), we start simply and then proceed to greater complexity, initially considering two values, then four and then more, juggling more and more variables in the process. In effect, in the same proactive spirit of our earlier work in this section, you are projecting an immense simplification into your subject. In the high contrast exercise, you represent a possibly infinite range of values with only two, and how you simplify these values—where you draw the line between them—is the key. In the manner of Hillmann's drawings, these contour lines must be articulate. Squinting as you look helps. It simplifies the range of value and aids focusing on the shapes of value areas.

The essence of this exercise is a figure-ground process of sorts, which parallels the work on a stone sculpture. Consider what is at stake for a sculptor. He starts with a stone. Then he chisels it away. You start with a white page. At the outset you have a

LIGHT AND DARK 2
Imposing Four Values on the Figure
1/4" brush, black, umber, ocher watercolor,
<u>*watercolor paper (low quality, ok).*</u>

Mix three colors, darkest (black), dark
(umber), light (ocher) so that, together with
the white page, they yield an even set of four
values from dark to light. Draw the model
with these four values. Using four values
allows more subtlety of range than was
available in the previous exercise, but you
still need to attend carefully to the break line
contours between values. These contour
lines articulate the form.

3.37 Above left: Riita Vepsalainen.
3.38 Hsien Chia Yu.

lot of it. Then you blacken it out, bit by bit. Just as a sculptor cannot put back the stone already carved away, as you proceed, you cannot reclaim the white space you have blackened. Once you've made an area black, it's black.

You both proceed by taking away from what you have, and you both must be cautious in similar ways. Just as the sculptor must be careful not to chisel away too much stone, lest he remove what ultimately should become a nose or a finger, you must take care lest you remove too much light.

The comparison applies to the end game as well. When the process works, what is left over in both cases takes on a figural meaning. The sculptor is left with a stone that becomes a human being. And you are left with white page that becomes light. And each material, stone or white page, takes on that figural meaning when just the right amount of each is left.

LIGHT AND DARK 3
Chiaroscuro
Black, white prismacolor, gray paper

In this exercise, we approach value from the middle of the value scale rather than from the end as we have previously done. Choose a piece of architectural sculpture with a variety of articulate shapes of dark and light and a sufficient range of value from dark to light. Working with white and black Prismacolor on gray charcoal paper, describe the full range of value on the surface of the sculpture. As you have previously done, proactively interpret the shapes of the areas of dark and light in such a way that they suggest form.

Build on previous exercises. Simplify at the outset to just three values: white, gray paper and black. Then expand this to five, all the while being attentive to the shape of the gray space. In this exercise blank page functions much as the white space did in previous exercises. It is a reciprocal, which must always remain in consideration.

3.39 Right: Teri Tsang.
3.40 Far right: Jaewoo You.

Working from the middle out

At the outset of the two previous exercises, on account of the media used, you started at the lighter end of the spectrum: the state of the untouched paper. And your analysis proceeded likewise in a parallel direction from light to dark. However, you can also work from the middle out. As in the exercise above, you only need to use a background, like the gray paper above, that lies somewhere near the middle of your value range.

You do not want to hurry a value study. In the exercise above, you cannot easily erase the prismacolor. You need to "hedge your bets," so to speak, by committing only gradually to the range of value. This analogy to playing poker is useful. Faced with opponents you've never played before at an evening's game, you adopt a wait-and-see approach at the outset. First you watch how they play. You need to know their strengths, weaknesses and tendencies before you bet your house. Drawing with values is a similar juggling act. Be cautious early and bold at the end.

3.41 Above: Cynthia Kress.
3.42 Right: Yu Hsien Chia.

CONTRAST OF VALUE

Value and color

We now make a seamless transition from black and white drawing to color drawing. To make it as easy as possible, we will use pastels on gray paper. At the outset you can use them as direct substitutes for the prismacolors you just used in a recent exercise.

We begin by simply observing that colors, in addition to their properties as hues, also have properties of value. Some are lighter and some are darker. If we take a traditional color wheel arranged with complementary colors opposite each other, then we observe that the colors at the bottom, blue and violet, are darker, and those at the top, orange and yellow, are lighter. The colors on the two sides, red and green, are in the middle. Laid out as a continuum of values from light to dark this scale is more or less so: yellow -yellow/orange -orange -yellow/green -red/orange -green -red -red/violet -blue/green -violet -blue -blue/violet.

As we proceed with pastel, some of the issues of the previous exercises still remain. Look for subjects with a substantial range of value. Remain proactive in your interpretation as well. Interpret color values so that the edges between color areas likewise draw

3.43 Left: Contrast of value. Paris, Las Vegas. Photo: Sarah Cooper.

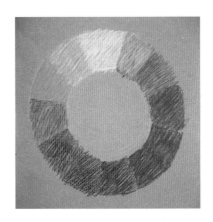

3.44 Above left: Yu Hsien Chia.
3.45 Above middle: Yu Hsien Chia.
3.46 Above right: Yellow is the lightest color, blue the darkest.

COLOR 1
Contrast of Value with pastels
Blue/violet, yellow/orange, gray paper.

Use two complementary colors with great difference in value between them: yellow/ orange and blue/violet. Substitute them in the same roles you gave white and black prismacolor in a previous exercise.

significant contours on the surface of your subjects. Just as a technical hint, I find an easy diagonal stroke (lower left to upper right if you are right handed) a good way to work quickly and at the same time achieve an atmospheric effect. Another approach is to use the page as a lighter value rather than in the middle. In you use this approach, work fairly monochromatically using the blue/violet as you used black in the previous exercise.

CONTRAST OF TEMPERATURE

Color temperature and color perspective

Color temperature is that attribute of color that we think of as warm or cool. Warm colors are reds and oranges. Cool colors are blues and greens. However, much as with the issue of value in the previous section, these are relative terms. Greens can be warm and reds can be cool. Consider the photograph I took at right on a cool winter morning when the sun was just starting to brighten a frosty area of grass. The shadow is a cool blue-green, but the sunlit area is a warm green.

It is said that "warm" colors tend to advance and that "cool" colors recede. This is not just the musing of interior decorators. There is a physiological basis for this effect related to one of the depth cues we discussed in Chapter 2. Remember the brief reference to accommodation (page 92)—when viewing near objects, muscles in the eyes slightly change the shape of the lens to focus an image clearly on the retina. The registration of this muscle action is what yields the sense of depth; we sense the nearness of things through the action of having to accommodate for them. It turns out that colors are focused at different distances and that some accommodation is necessary to focus them on the retina. It also turns out that for "warm" colors, colors in the red and orange part of the spectrum, the muscular action of accommodation is similar to the action used to focus near objects. The parallel in the muscular action is the basis for "color perspective."[9]

Color perspective can be used to dramatically draw attention to background areas. We've experienced this before earlier in the book: the figure ground exercises of Chapter 1 where we drew the spaces between the bones of the dinosaur skeletons (page 61). There we attended to the spaces between the bones and ignored the bones themselves.

3.48 A normally cool color, green, can be either cool or warm. Carnegie Mellon University campus.

---

[9] Libby, William Charles. *Color and the Structural Sense* (Englewood Cliffs, NJ: Prentice-Hall, Inc., 1974) pp. 67–68.

3.47 Opposite: It is said that warm colors tend to advance. Edwin Austin Abby. American, 1852–1911. *The Penance of Eleanor, Duchess of Glouchester.* 1900. Oil on canvas. 49" x 85". Carnegie Museum of Art, Pittsburgh, PA.: Purchase 02.1.

COLOR 2

Color Temperature and Color Perspective
Red/orange, blue, gray paper.

Find an architectural scene with significant and well-articulated depth. A layered scene with interesting overlaps will serve well. Represent the depth in the scene as an issue of color temperature. Use red and orange to advance some areas. Use blue to let other areas recede. If you wish, use gray paper as a neutral condition.

In subsequent drawings where you use more complex palettes, return regularly to the idea of an assertive background (as for example in Figure 3.49).

3.49 Andrew Kikta.

3.50 Tim Thianthai.

3.51 Ben Saks and Jared Langevin.

Parallel to that treatment, the warm colors used for the window in the pastel above cause that background area to become the composition's more assertive element.

In some cases background spaces can even seem to jump forward in a figure/ground reversal of sorts. The previous page shows Edwin Austin Abbey's *The Penance of Eleanor*, based on Shakespeare's Henry VII. It shows Eleanor being forced to walk barefoot through the streets of London in punishment for her treachery against the King. And in a wonderful parallel to the story's narrative, the warm reds used for the men guarding her seem to almost push her forward through the street. Color perspective can also be subtle. In a recent design presentation drawing, two former students of mine (Figure 3.51) used warm Prismacolor to activate the spaces between the trees in the forested site that surrounds their building proposal. The effect is airy, active and alive!

3.52 Derek Rubinoff.

Color temperature and mood of light
<u>*Pastels on gray paper.*</u>

Draw an architectural scene with a definite mood; a room at sunset, an interior with garish light as at left, or a room with a distant warm light source would be good examples.

3.53 Unknown artist.

Temperature and mood

Light and color can carry different moods. We associate different colors with different seasons, times of day, and their related moods. Light off of a snowy surface is often "cooler." Light from a fireplace is "warmer."

Our ability to see colors at various times of day influences the moods we associate with them. In fact, we do not see all colors equally under all conditions of light. Under the low light levels of evening, blue is the color we are still most able to see. The other colors tend to retire. This is the reason why moonlight seems so rendered in blue. It is also perhaps why "the blues" are so tied to the moods of night and not day. The exercise above is directed at such temperature differences and the moods they produce. In it we try to create a sense of garishness, or joy, or sadness, or longing.

COMPLEMENTARY CONTRAST

What are complements?

Complementary colors are balanced opposites. When mixed with each other, they cancel each other out. Red mixed with its complement green results in a gray of sorts called a "chromatic gray." Placed next to each other, complements set each other off: blue in the presence of orange in the photo in Bryce Canyon at left, yellows in the presence of violets in the drawing at right. Red and green seem particularly vibrant in the presence of the other. Every redhead knows to wear green and blue sweaters.

Complementary contrast is a powerful effect. Several years ago, I had cataracts removed. After the patch was removed from the first eye and while my wife was driving me home, all the colors in the blue/violet range seemed astonishingly vibrant. That night I remember looking out into the night at some newly fallen snow. The light from the street looked its usual warm orange, but the shadow cast by the tree was a vibrant blue/violet. What I experienced that evening was complementary contrast at a fever pitch!

For months I had been viewing the world through the yellow of the cataracts. Acting as a filter, the cataracts had in effect cancelled yellow's complement, violet, out of my vision. Now with their removal, I was ultra-sensitive to violet, and for several days I walked through a world awash in violet.

I have said that complements balance each other. But I use the word balance in the dynamic sense of two children at opposite ends of a teeter-totter. The one *with* the other results in a playful balance. The one without the other lacks vitality. After all, how long would any child sit on a teeter-totter without a partner at the other end?

3.55 Yu Hsien Chia.

3.54 Opposite: Placed next to each other complementary colors set each other off: blue in the presence of orange for example. Rainy Day in Bryce Canyon. Photo: Sarah Cooper.

3.56 Left: Yu Hsien Chia.
3.57 Below: Andrew Kitka.

COLOR 4

Complementary contrast
<u>*Pastels on gray paper*</u>
Draw an architectural scene, which has various material properties: bricks tiles, wood etc. Develop a simple set of complementary pairs with which to develop the scene.

Complementary palettes may be simple complements. Red/violet vs. yellow/orange would be an example. Or they may be split complements against one another. As you work, set out your colors in a systematic way. The drawing by Andrew above balances orange with its complement blue, and violet with its complement yellow. The drawing by Yu Hsien at the left uses red and green as one pair and blue-violet and yellow-orange as another. A third possibility, one which is interesting for its slightly off-center chromatic grays, is to set a single color off against a pair of colors—one on either side of its true complement.

WHAT'S THE NEXT STEP?

We have now looked at the subject of architectural drawing from three very distinct understandings of perceptual theory: 1) affirming a relationship to touch as well as vision, 2) analyzing the order already present in the visual environment, and 3) in this chapter considering the order we might bring to the process. "But where," you might ask, "do I go from here? How might these understandings of perception and their relationship to drawing impact the kind of drawings I'll need to make in designing?"

A example using an early point in the design process

Let's consider the kind of circumstance you often find yourelf in: a vague idea early on in a design project, no idea of what to do next (other than talk), and a board critique four hours away. The advice I offer is this: draw now, talk later. After you get the hang of them (which comes from doing them often), drawings like the ones in the presentation that follows should take you no more than four hours to complete. And the quality of the design critique you'll provoke and the insights into your idea you'll gain as a result of such a thorough (and efficient) presentation will be well worth the time spent.

Let's say you are designing a small house, and your first sketch looks something like the drawing at right. It's just the tickle of an idea, but note that I'm representing it in a *set* of multiple diagrammatic drawings: not just a quick plan, but a quick section too. Notice the line character of these drawings as well. They have something of the gestural quality of our exercises on that topic in Chapter 1. These are not stiff drawings made of stick-like lines. These lines flow! It is out of a desire to be actively engaging these drawings—interacting with them in the spirit of that chapter—that I have drawn them this way. In the manner of the contour drawings we did then, by keeping my hand moving, my eyes are also engaged. They come along for the ride. With that in mind, note the lines that seem to move down along the corridor. I was imagining myself moving through that space when I drew them.

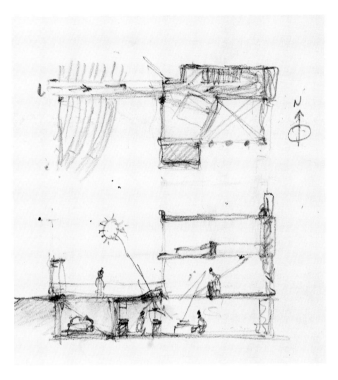

3.58 Notice the gestural quality of the lines. Preliminary drawings of a house.

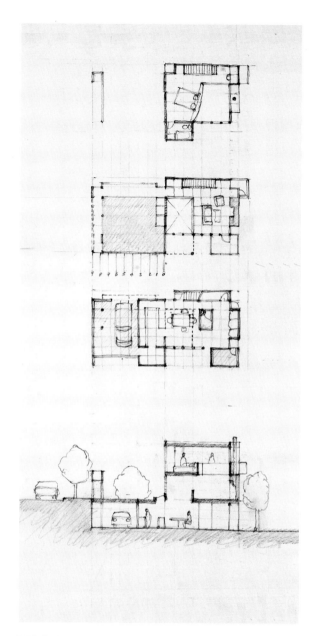

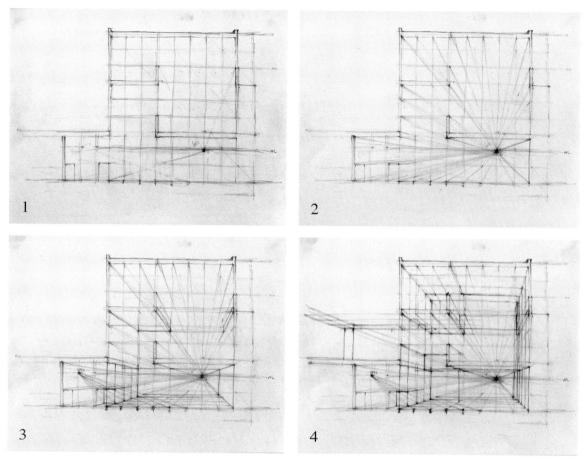

1

2

3

4

3.59 Preliminary plans and sections.
3.60-3.63 Above right: Magic method Steps 1–4.

In the next set of drawings (see Figure 3.59), size becomes a more compelling consideration. In the spirit of Chapter 3, I project order into the drawings by using a grid. This grid does not necessarily represent a construction or planning grid. Its primary purpose (somewhat like graph paper) is to give the drawings an easy measurability. By drawing them in this way (think of Gibson's perspective order) I can then more quickly develop the set of perspectives that follows: a sectional view and a two-point interior.

One-point sectional perspective

I've chosen to do a longitudinal section of this early proposal because it explains much about the relationships among the several levels in the house and shows something of

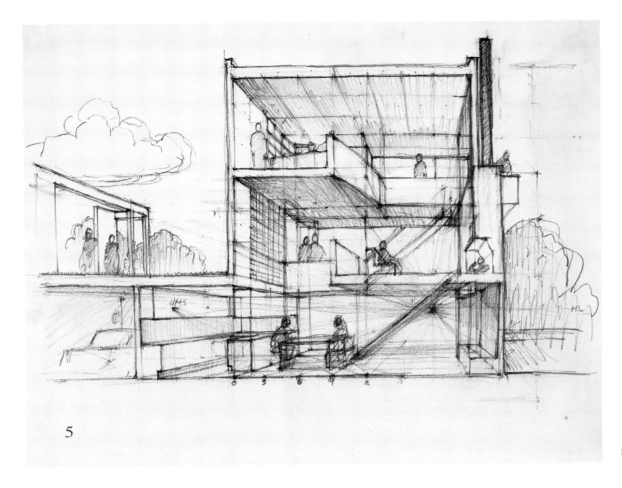

5

3.64 Magic method Step 5.

the building's relationship to site: it's on a hill. To do it I need only use the section I've already drawn as a forward wall picture plane, and I'll extrude the space backward from there. I'll use soft precise lines for the armature and heavier and more varied lines for line-work over top of the armature. Here are the steps I'll follow:

1) Pick a central vanishing point.
2) Extrude longitudinal lines backward.
3) Find the vanishing point of a 45°, and lay out a scale along the inside base line.
4) Build the spatial armature.
5) Develop the architecture over top (include furniture).

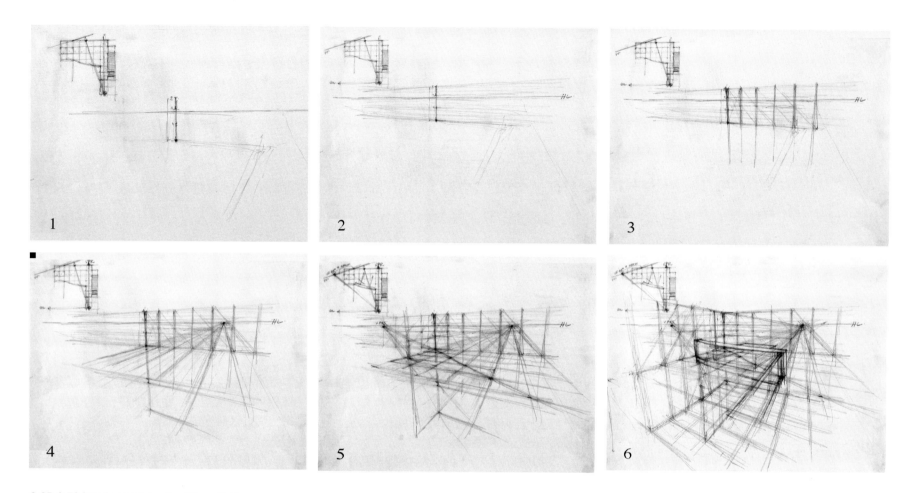

3.65-3.70 Interior perspective Steps 1–6

Two-point slightly inclined view

A two-point view from the top floor offers the prospect (more than the sectional perspective) of showing a sense of what it might be like to be in this house. Because of the smallness of the house and its degree of verticality, I'm going to converge the verticals slightly downward as I draw them, yielding a view that gives a slight sense of looking downward. Other than that, the construction will be the same as previous interior one-point views, and I'll use the same kind of line work—armature to finished drawing—I've used previously.

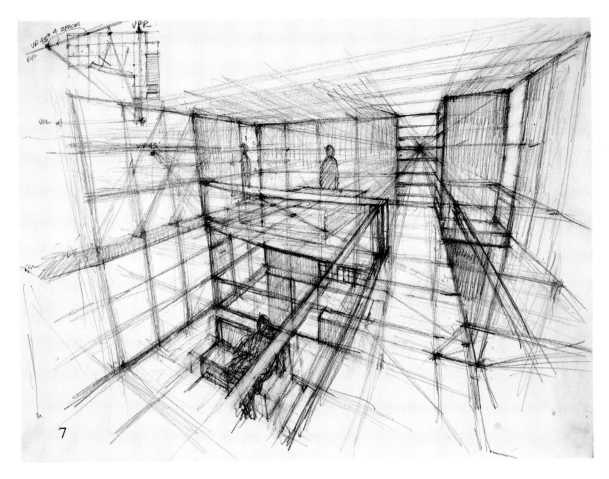

3.71 Interior perspective Step 7.

1) Draw a corner and a horizon line at the viewer's height.

2) Develop a vanishing point for the end wall of the space and converge lines to it.

3) Represent one end wall grid interval and extend it along the end wall.

4) Find the vanishing point for longitudinal lines (lines perpendicular to your end-wall grid), and bring these forward.

5) Find a vanishing point for a 45°, and draw diagonals across the floor grid to develop increments of foreshortening.

6) Build the spatial armature.

7) Develop the architecture over top (include furniture).

Appendices

APPENDIX A
PERSPECTIVE: OFFICE METHOD

The first method for constructing perspectives using plans and elevations is usually attributed to Piero della Francesca (1420?–1492). It is also possible that Paolo Uccello (1397–1475) might have developed a method as well. Whoever the originator was, the ability to work from orthographic drawings made it possible for the first time to generate views of objects of any shape from any direction. Alberti's method of grids had enabled only frontal or 45° views and was difficult to use with nonrectangular objects. Over the years, one of the codified methods derived from the early perspectivists came to be called the "office method." It is this method that is presented here.

We generate perspective views by projecting an image of a subject to or through a picture plane using sight lines. In the office method we use two separate orthographic views. We use a plan showing the construction from above to enter information about the location of the viewer and the shape, location and orientation of the objects in the scene. We use an elevation (or section) for information about the height of the viewer's standpoint and the heights of those same objects. We use these two views in combination, bringing them together on the picture plane to form the actual perspective.

A.1 Opposite: David Celento.

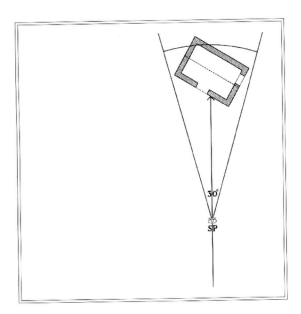

A.2 Office Method Step 1.

1: Locating the station point

As I stated earlier, perspective is unique among drawing systems in that it yields the view from one individual and singular point in space. We begin the construction process with the location of that unique point called the "station point."

1.1 Determine the desired direction or line of sight from which you will view the building (frontal, lateral, etc.). Then position the plan accordingly with the line of sight represented with a vertical line on your drawing board.

1.2 Decide how much of the building you want to show. Do you want to show the whole building, in which case you would want to stand further away, or do you want to show a detail of the building, in which case you would want to stand closer?

1.3 Locate the station point (SP) along the line of sight. It should be positioned far enough away from the building so you can fit whatever about the building you want to show within a reasonable cone of vision (breadth of field). For most uses a reasonable cone of vision can be as great as 60°. In the example at right a more conservative 30° cone of vision has been used.

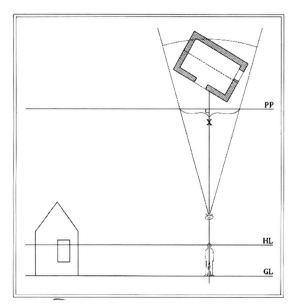

A.3 Office Method Step 2.

2: Locating the picture plane

It is on the picture plane that we construct a perspective. We locate the picture plane in this way.

2.1 First you need to determine the size of the view. You might base this decision on: 1) the size of available paper, 2) the medium to be used and its implications as to size, 3) the level of detail desirable in the view, and 4) the distances from which the drawing is to be viewed.

2.2 Then position the picture plane (PP) in the plan so that the picture plane intercepts your cone of vision at a width x equal to your desired width for the view. Remember, the picture plane must be perpendicular to your line of sight.

2.3 Square to the line of sight and to the left (or right) of the area where you will draw the perspective, position an elevation or section of the building. Then, at appropriate heights on that elevation, draw horizontals representing the ground line (GL) and the horizon line (HL). The horizon line represents the height of the viewer's eye. Draw it to scale at that height the viewer's eye is located above the ground.

3: Locating vanishing points

It is by using vanishing points that perspectives achieve their sense of depth. Locate vanishing points for sets of horizontal lines with this procedure.

3.1 In plan, draw lines parallel to the sets of lines (side A and side B) for which you want to find vanishing points. These lines should be drawn from the station point (SP) out to points of intersection with the picture plane (PP).

3.2 Transfer these points of intersection with the picture plane (PP) to equivalent positions on the horizon line (HL). These resultant points are the vanishing points for the two sides of the building, vanishing point left (VPL) for side A and vanishing point right (VPR) for side B.

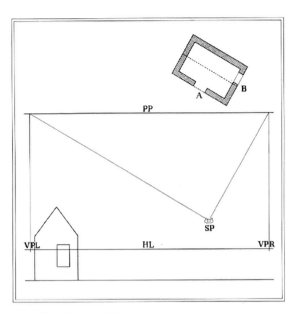

A.4 Office Method Step 3.

4: Vertical line of measure

While perspectives are not scaled drawings used to represent true dimensions, we still draw them with reference to the true sizes of objects. In positioning the plan, picture plane and station point, we have already entered the true widths, depths, and locations of objects into our perspective drawing. But entering vertical information is somewhat more complicated.

We enter it by first generating an auxiliary line called the "vertical line of measure." Because the picture plane is the only location where we can draw to scale, we must locate this line on the picture plane. Sometimes this is easy. If the object already intersects the picture plane, we need only use that line of intersection directly. However, if the object is behind or in front of the picture plane, then we must extend one of its planes until it intersects the picture plane. We develop the vertical information there and then transfer it to the object using the appropriate vanishing points. Since the house in our view dies not already intersect the picture plane, we have to extend one of its planes forward.

4.1 In plan, extend side A to a point of intersection with the picture plane (PP). (If side A had already intersected the picture plane, you could have proceeded directly to step 4.2.)

4.2 Project that point of intersection vertically down the drawing until it crosses both the horizon line (HL) and the ground line (GL). This vertical line is the vertical line of measure (VLM). (If side A had already intersected the picture plane, you would have merely projected the VLM from that point of intersection.)

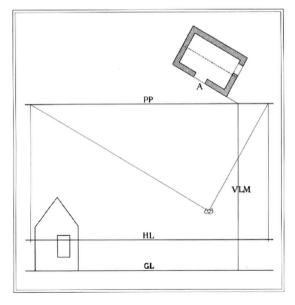

A.5 Office Method Step 4.

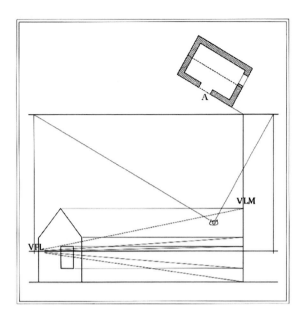

A.6 Office Method Step 5.

5: Entering vertical information

Usually we enter vertical information by using a preexisting section or elevation such as the one already positioned in the drawing at right. The process is one of merely projecting that information over to the vertical line of measure (VLM).

5.1 From relevant points on the elevation of side A or side B, project horizontals to points of intersection with the vertical line of measure (VLM).

5.2 From these points of intersection, converge this vertical information to the vanishing point of side A (VPL).

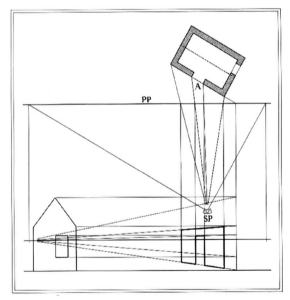

A.7 Office Method Step 6.

6: Constructing one face

You now have sufficient vertical information to construct the perspective of the building. Begin by representing one face of the building. Then use this part to generate the rest. Side A can serve this purpose. Because you have already generated the information about its heights (step 5.2), you can immediately begin to sight its lateral information: its two ends and the location of the door.

6.1 In plan, sight relevant points along side A to points of intersection with the picture plane. Draw sightlines from the station point back through the picture plane to points on the wall. Where these sightlines cross the picture plane, draw vertical lines.

6.2 Use these vertical lines in concert with the convergent lines on side A to complete the perspective view of side A.

7: Completing the perspective

Now you start to address some of the other planes of the object. From the roof peak, base and edges of side A, converge lines to VPR. These will start to set the information necessary to establish these other planes.

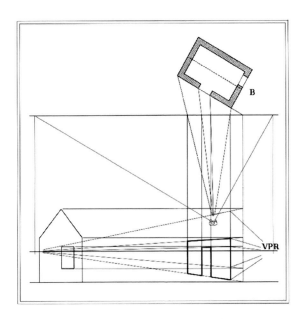

A.8 Office Method Step 7.

8: Completing the perspective

You only have a few remaining lines to draw. Construct side B and the roof planes. In plan, sight relevant points along side B to points of intersection with the picture plane. Draw sightlines from the station point back through the picture plane to points on the house. Where these sightlines cross the picture plane, project lines directly to the perspective view and flesh out the view accordingly.

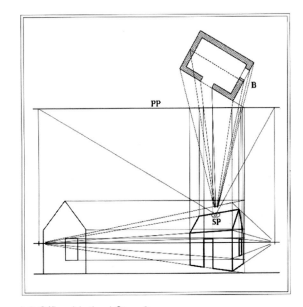

A.9 Office Method Step 8.

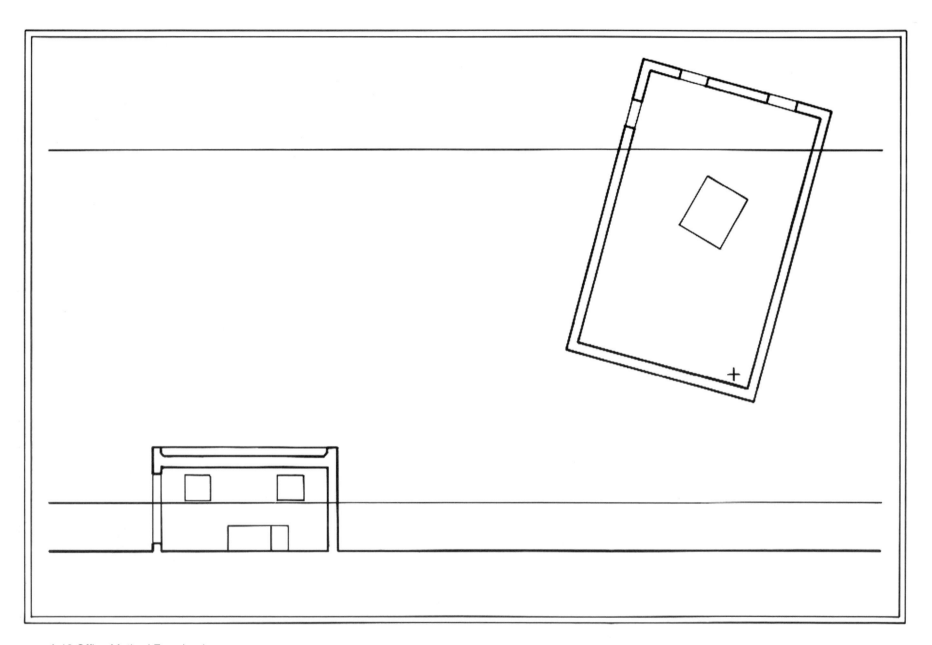

A.10 Office Method Exercise 1.

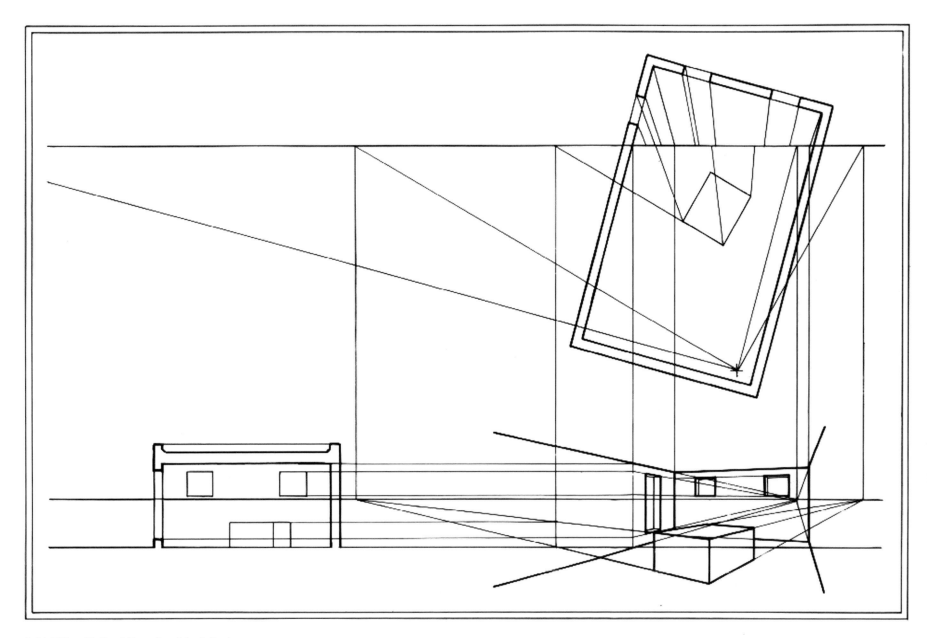

A.11 Office Method Exercise 1 (solution).

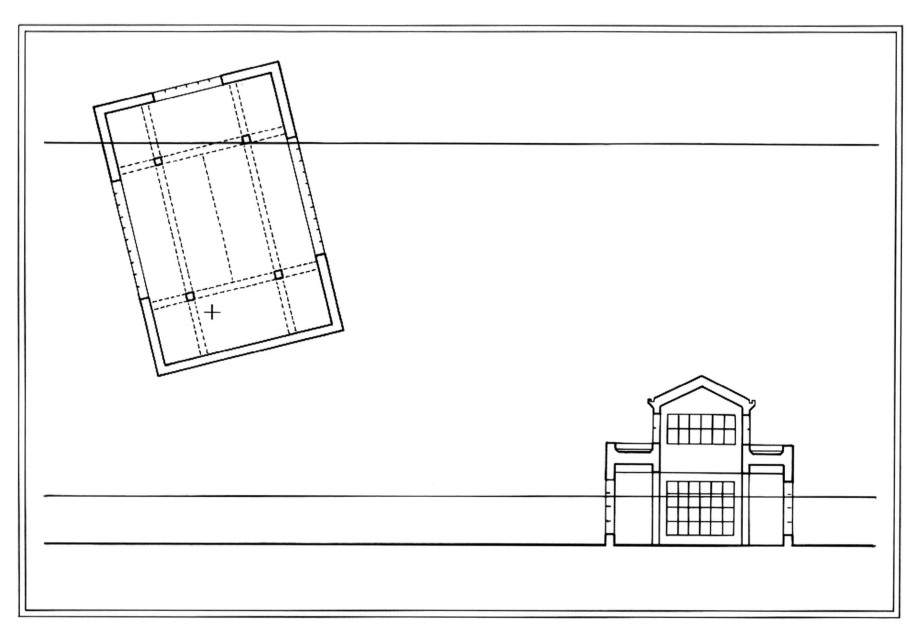

A.12 Office Method Exercise 2.

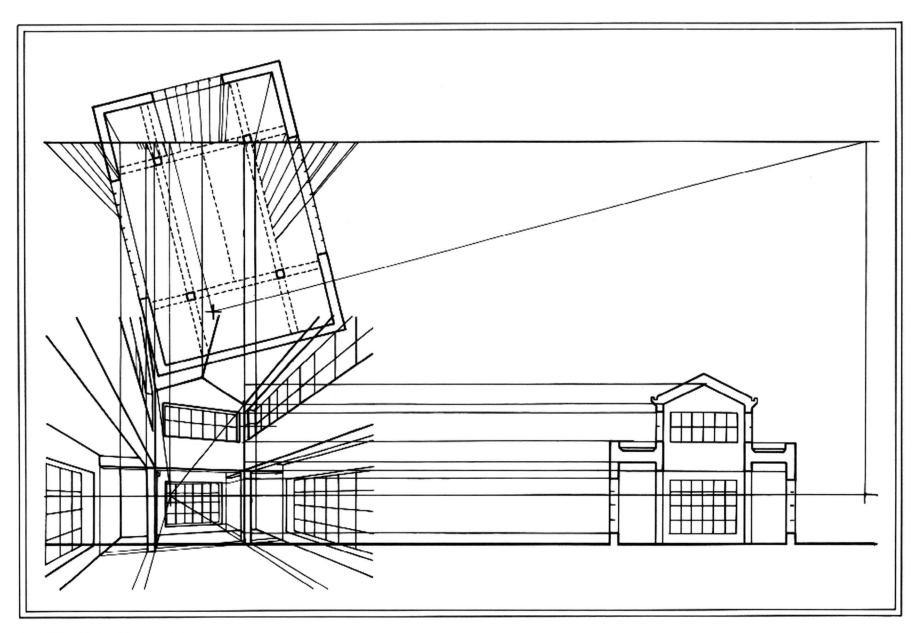

A.13 Office Method Exercise 2 (solution).

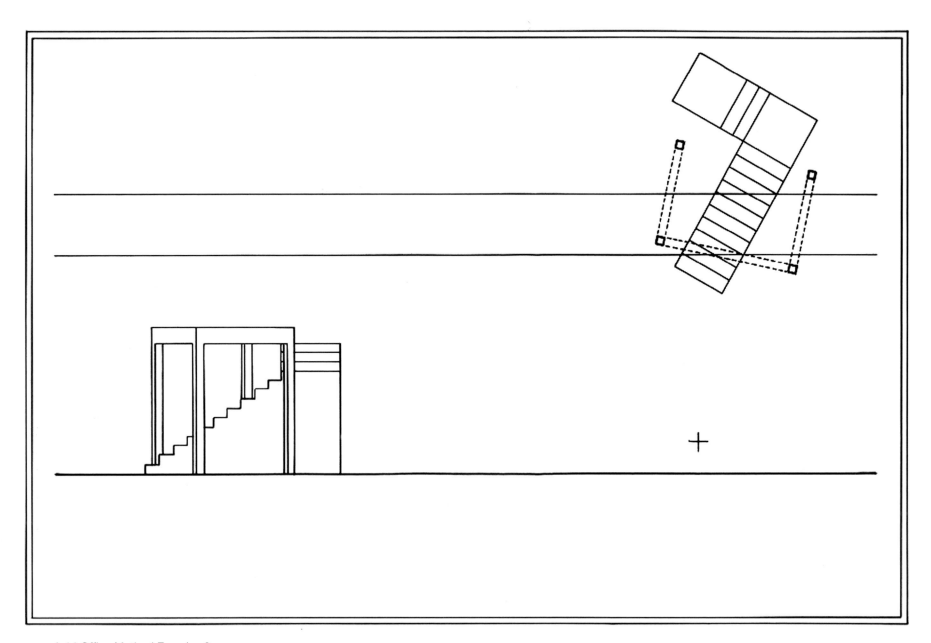

A.14 Office Method Exercise 3.

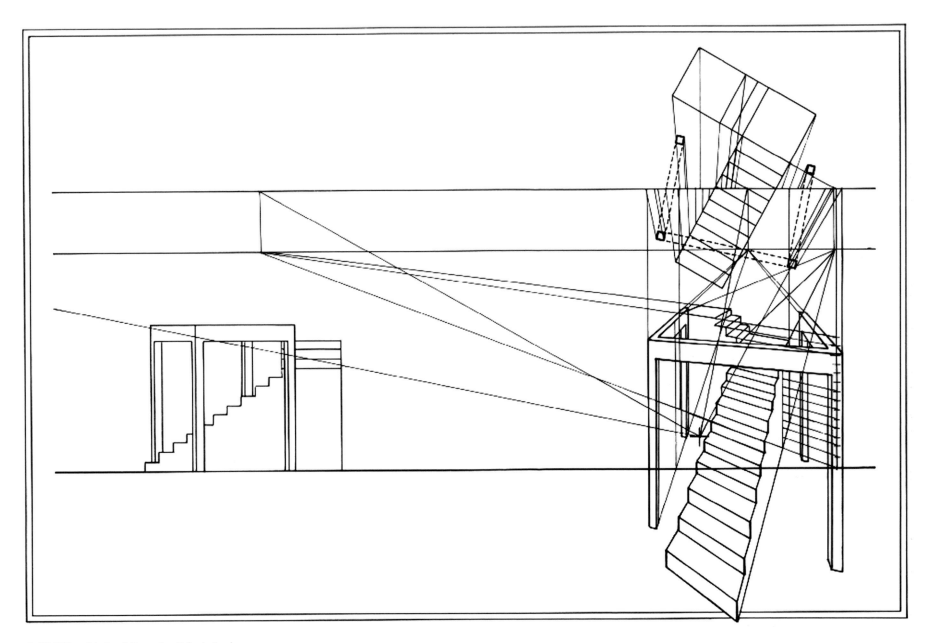

A.15 Office Method Exercise 3 (solution).

APPENDIX B
ONE-POINT MAGIC METHOD[1]

Using a one-point construction called the "magic method," we can dispense altogether with the process of sighting on plans and generating vertical lines of measure. This method is based on Alberti's system, the *Construzione Leggitima,* from the mid-fifteenth century. That method had concluded a long search for an accurate method to determine foreshortening. Though limited effectively to one-point perspective views, the magic method is enormously useful exactly because it is so simple. It is used to rapidly test design proposals early in the design process (see pages 180–181).

The magic method is based on the fact that the vanishing point of a 45° spatial diagonal must be the same distance (to the left or right of the central vanishing point) as the viewer is standing from the picture plane. This owes to the fact that 45° triangles have sides of equal length. We are able to locate this point, the vanishing point for a 45° line, without using a station point or projecting lines to the picture plane. We merely lay it out directly on the picture plane (for which an existing section or elevation is conveniently used) by measuring to the left or right of the central vanishing point the distance of the viewer from the picture plane. We then use this vanishing point to measure distances out from or back from the picture plane. There are two types of magic views. One uses an end-wall elevation for its picture plane, the other a cross-section.

---

[1] Kevin Forseth, *Graphics for Architecture* (New York: Van Nostrand Reinhold Co., 1980) pp. 140–142

B.1 Opposite: Andrew Kikta.

Interior from an elevation

1: Draw ground and horizon lines (GL, HL).

2: Locate central vanishing point (VP).

3: Locate vanishing point for diagonal (VPD) left or right of VP.

4: Use VP to vanish edges of floor, ceiling, and other relevant points out from the elevation.

5: Construct a horizontal measuring line (HML) located along the ground line so that zero (no depth from the elevation) is at the lower left or right outside corner of the elevation.

6: Use HML together with VPD to project increments of depth to the right or left edge of the floor, and project these points out into the interior of the room.

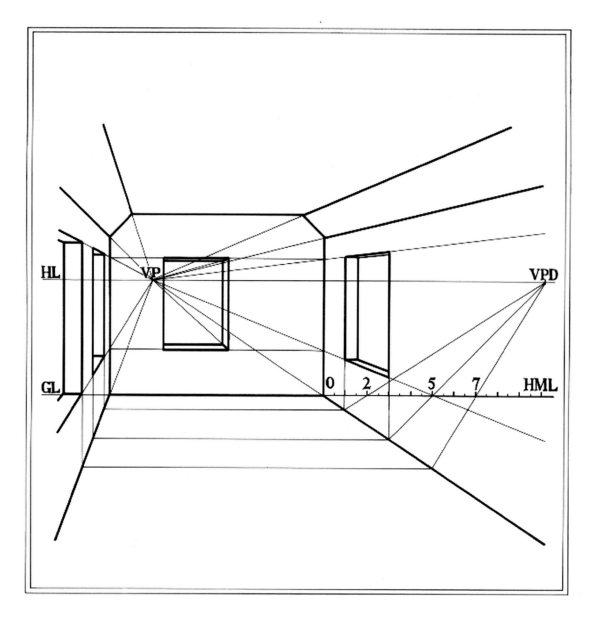

B.2 Magic Method using an end-wall elevation.

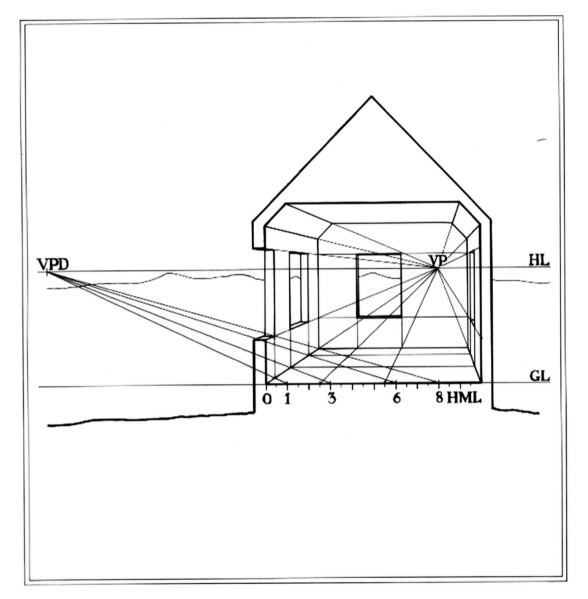

Interior from a section

1: Draw ground and horizon lines (GL, HL).

2: Locate the central vanishing point (VP).

3: Locate the vanishing point for the diagonal (VPD) left or right of VP.

4: Vanish edges of ceilings, floors, walls, and other relevant points from the section back toward the VP.

5: Construct a horizontal measuring line (HML). HML should be located along the ground line so that zero (no depth from the section) is at the lower left or right inside corner of the section. Use HML together with VPD to project increments of depth to the right or left edge of floor, and project these points out into the interior of the room.

B.3 Magic Method using a section.

APPENDIX C
SHADOW PROJECTION
IN ORTHOGRAPHIC VIEWS[1]

The Appendices conclude with the study of shade and shadow projection, first in orthographic projection and finally in perspective. Shadow casting always used to be included in courses on projective geometry. However, with the arrival of the computer, it is no longer necessary to construct shadows by hand, and the subject is no longer taught. This is unfortunate because shadow casting was never just a tool. Its significance was (and remains) as a hurdle to teach and test capabilities of three-dimensional visualization. Shadow casting in orthographic projection requires construction over a set of drawings, usually a plan and an elevation, and cross-referencing information back and forth between them.

We'll start with a few principles of the process. There is a single convention for the direction of light in orthographic projection. In plan, it is represented by a line slanting at 45° toward the upper right. In elevation, it is represented by a line slanting down at an angle of 45° down to the lower right. Effectively the convention represents light following the path of the spatial diagonal of a cube.

In developing the shadow we'll use a process of passing a vertical plane through the object receiving the shadow. This plane is called the "slice." Consider it to be much like the plane that would result if you were to cut through the object receiving the shadow with the vertical stroke of a broad knife.

---

[1] Adapted from: Maxwell G. Mayo, *Line and Light* (Pittsburgh: Department of Architecture, Carnegie Mellon University, 1971) Chapters 1–9.

C.1 Opposite: Shade and shadow in orthographic projection.

1: Casting the shadow of a point, the slicing method

To cast the shadow of a point in orthographic projection, pass a vertical plane through the point and the object or surface receiving the shadow. This is a four-step process starting in plan, then moving to the elevation and finally returning to the plan.

1.1 Draw the vertical plane first in plan. Conveniently, it will always be represented with a straight line at 45°. The shadow of the point must lie somewhere along this plan of the slice.

1.2 Next, through a process of transferring relevant points from the plan of the slice to corresponding points on the objects in the elevation, develop an elevation view of the slice line. The shadow of the point must lie somewhere along this elevation of the slice.

1.3 Then, in the elevation, cast a ray of sunlight through the point and extend it to a point of intersection with the elevation of the slice. This point of intersection is the shadow of the point in elevation.

1.4 Finally, with a vertical line transfer this point from the elevation to the plan of the slice in the plan view. This point of intersection is the shadow of the point in plan.

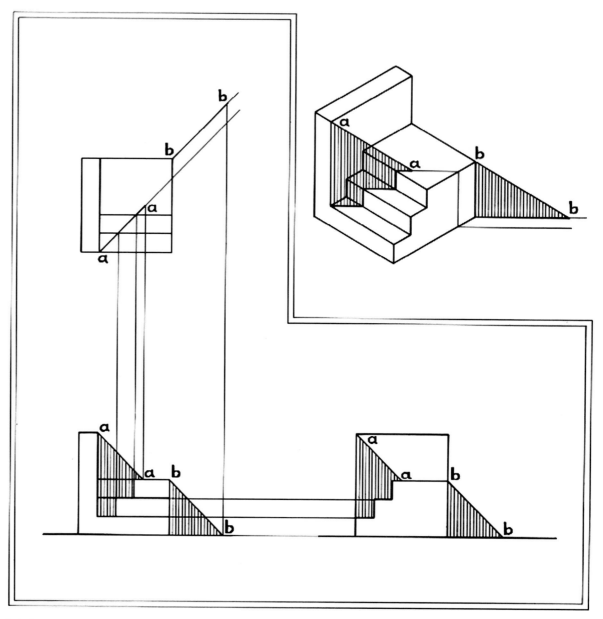

C.2 Casting the shadow of a point, the slicing method.

2: Casting the shadow of a solid

To cast the shadow of a solid, the shadows of the solid's vertices are found via the slicing method and then connected.

C.3 Casting the shadow of a solid.

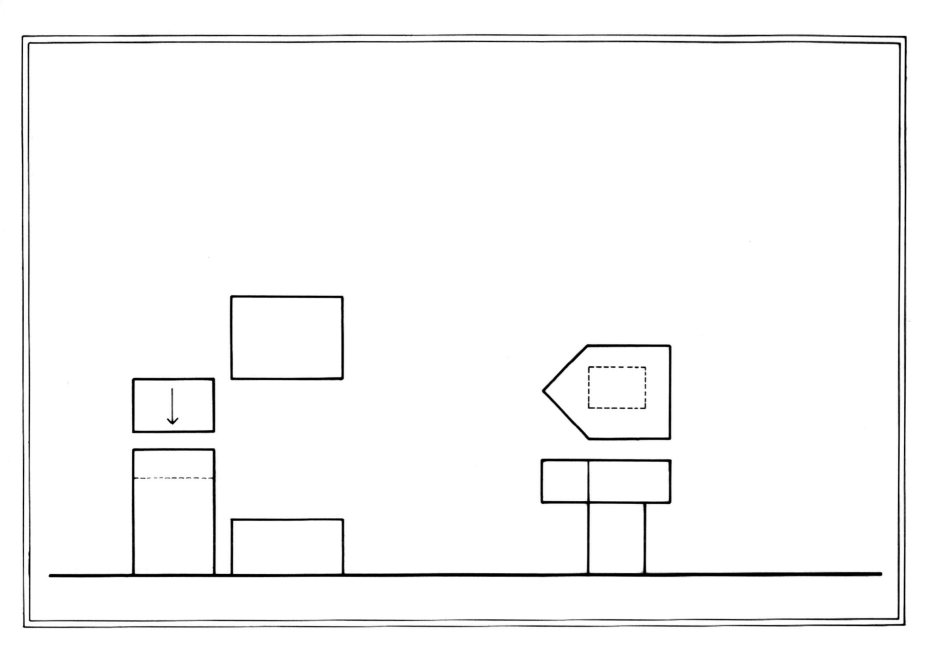

C.4 Shade and shadow in orthographic projection, Exercise 1.

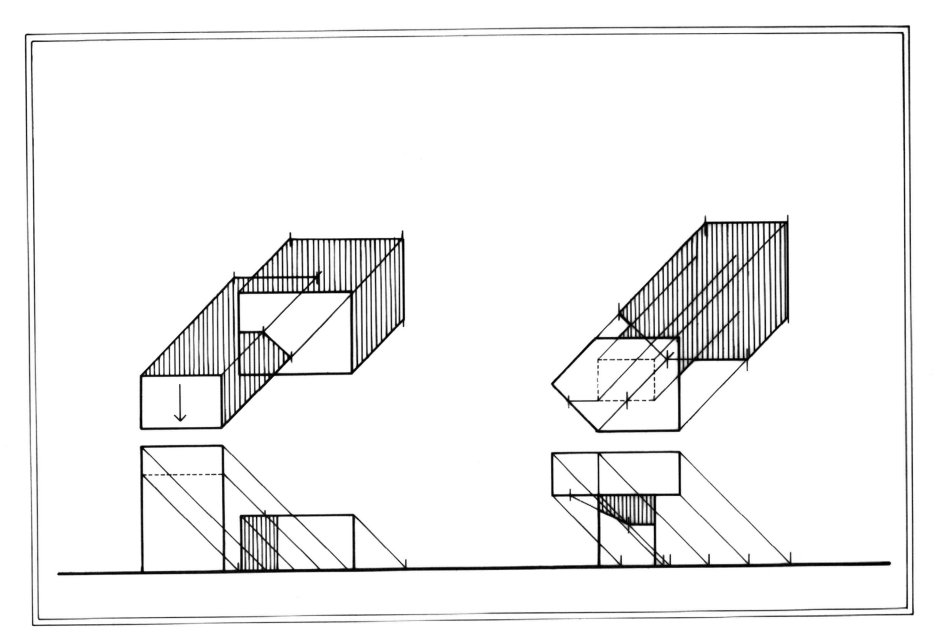

C.5 Shade and shadow in orthographic projection, Exercise 1 (solution).

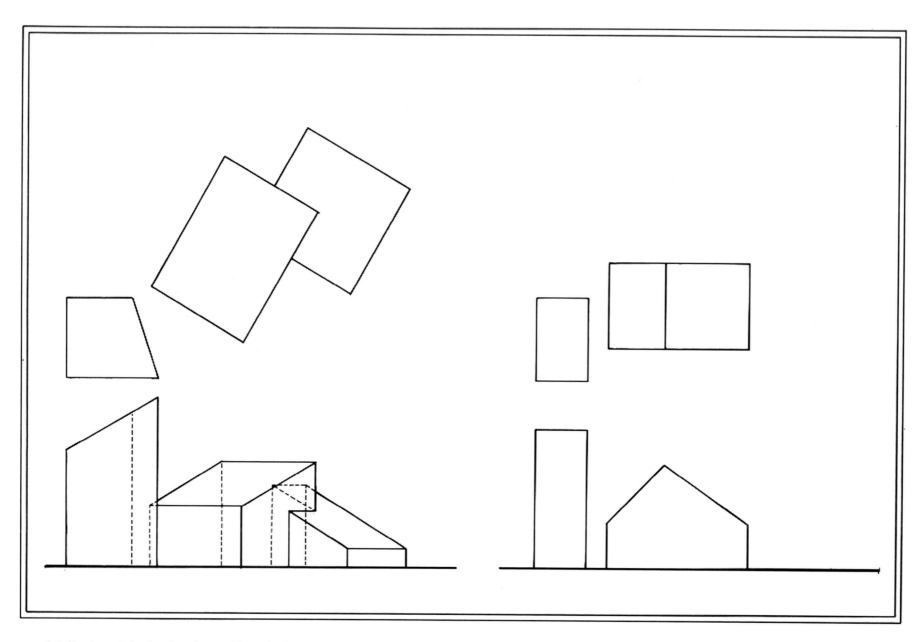

C.6 Shade and shadow in orthographic projection, Exercise 2.

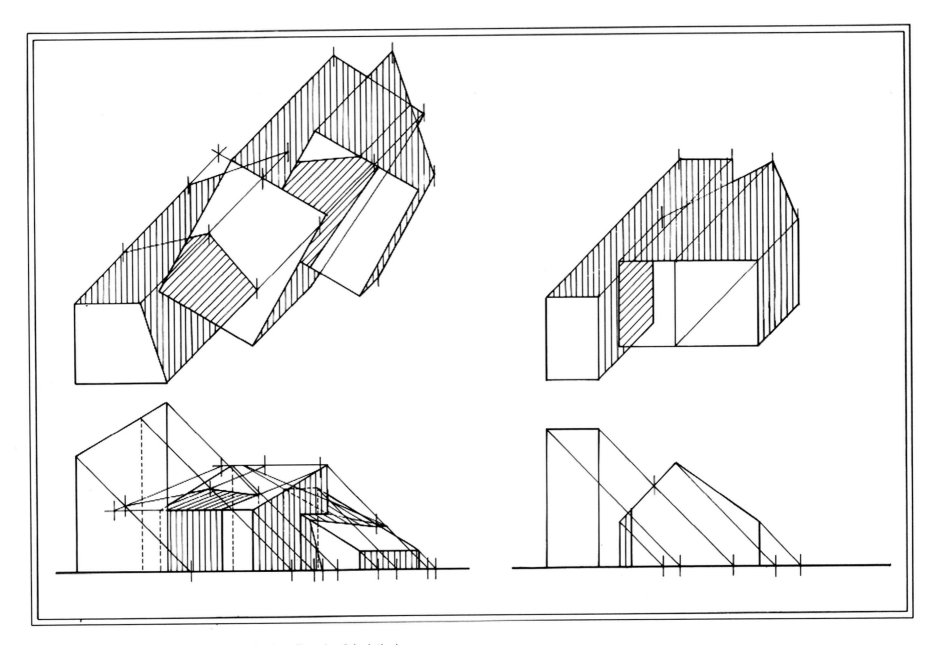

C.7 Shade and shadow in orthographic projection, Exercise 2 (solution).

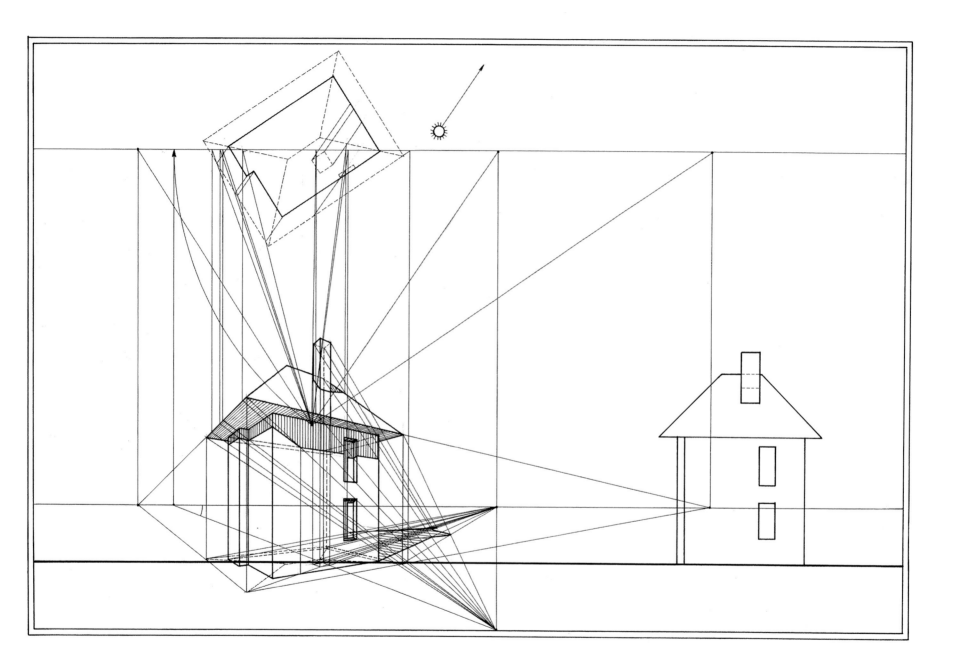

APPENDIX D
SHADOW PROJECTION
IN PERSPECTIVE VIEWS[1]

The key to shadow projection in perspective is generating the vanishing point for a sloping line, the ray, and generating the vanishing point for the horizontal components of the slice line. These are issues we have encountered already when we drew stairs. There we found the vanishing point for their horizontal components—their risers and landings—and directly above or below that (depending on whether the stair was sloping up and away from us or down and away from us) we located the vanishing point for their sloping elements: their stringers and banisters. As we proceed, consider the vanishing point for the latter (the vanishing point for the banisters) as equivalent to the vanishing point for the ray, and the former (the vanishing point for the risers) as equivalent to the vanishing point for the slice line.

---

[1] Adapted from: Maxwell G. Mayo, *Line and Light* (Pittsburgh: Department of Architecture, Carnegie Mellon University, 1971) pp. 1–9.

D.1 Opposite: Shade and shadow in perspective projection.

1: Locate vanishing point of slice line

This is the same construction we used before in finding the vanishing point for an angled wall. Because the horizontal components of the slice line are parallel to the ground, their shared vanishing point must lie along the horizon line.

1.1 Draw a line from the SP parallel to the sun's ray to a point of intersection with the picture plane. This is the vanishing point for the slice line (in plan).

1.2 Transfer this point to the horizon line (VP Slice).

2: Close the door

We consider the line from the station point to the vanishing point of the slice line as a door of sorts and rotate it so it lies flat on the picture plane. We do this so we can construct the slope of the sun's ray on the picture plane, the one location in a perspective where we can draw to scale.

2.1 Set one end of a compass at the vanishing point for the slice line (VP Slice) and extend it out to the station point (SP).

2.2 Circle an arc through the station point (SP) to the picture plane (PP), in effect representing the station point on the picture plane (SP').

2.3 Transfer this point to the horizon line (SP"). This point represents the position of the viewer both on the picture plane and on the horizon line.

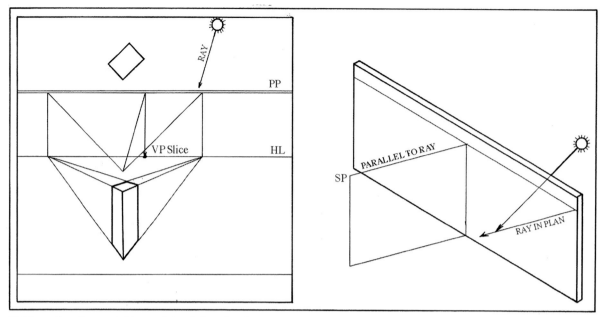

D.2 Locating the vanishing points of the slice line.

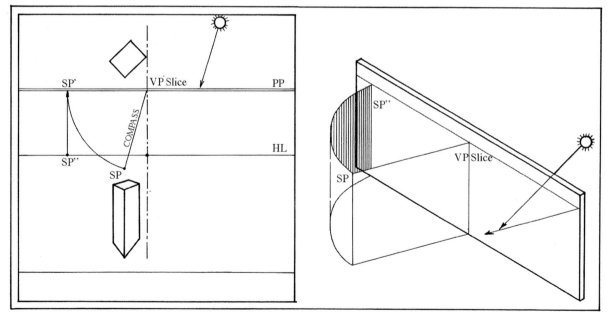

D.3 Closing the door.

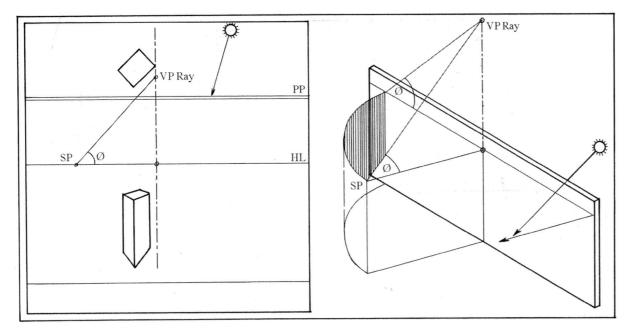

D.4 Locating the vanishing point of the ray.

3: Locate the vanishing point of the ray

3.1 At this point (SP"), draw the angle of the slope of the sun's ray ø. If the sun is coming down toward the viewer (as in the example here), this angle is erected above the horizon line. If the sun were at the viewer's back, the angle would be erected below the horizon line.

3.2 Draw a vertical through the vanishing point for the slice line. As with the vanishing point for sloping stairs, the vanishing point of the ray must lie along this line.

3.3 Extend the angle of the sun's ray ø up to (or down to) a point of intersection with this vertical line. This is the vanishing point for the sun's ray (VP Ray).

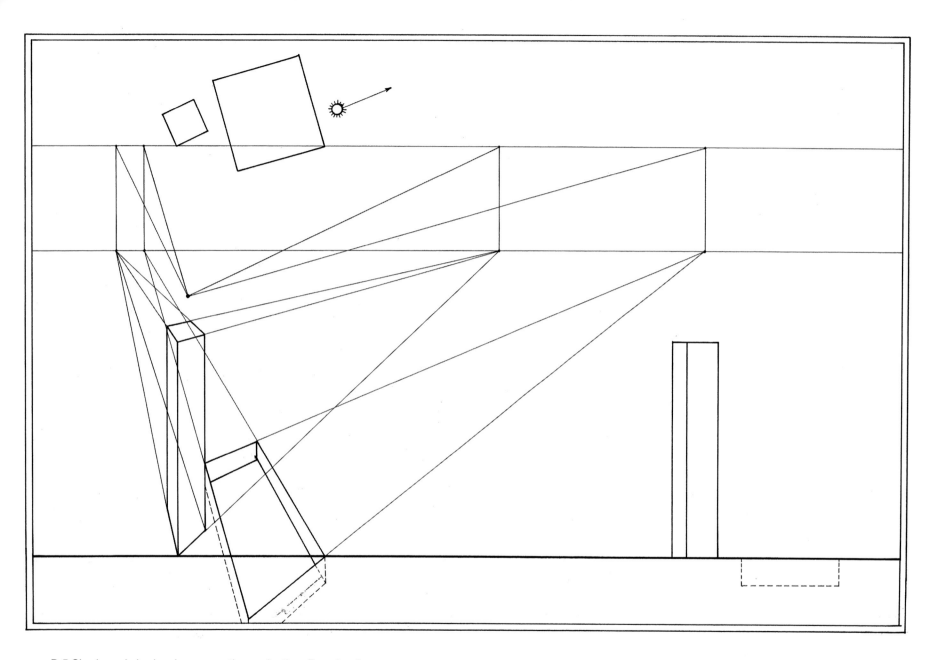

D.5 Shade and shadow in perspective projection, Exercise 1.

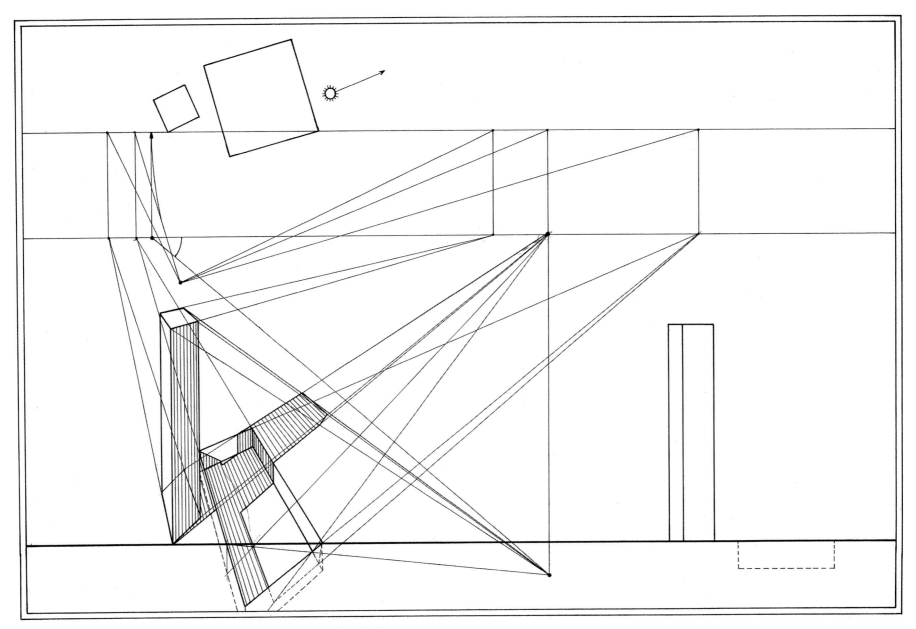

D.6 Shade and shadow in perspective projection, Exercise 1 (solution).

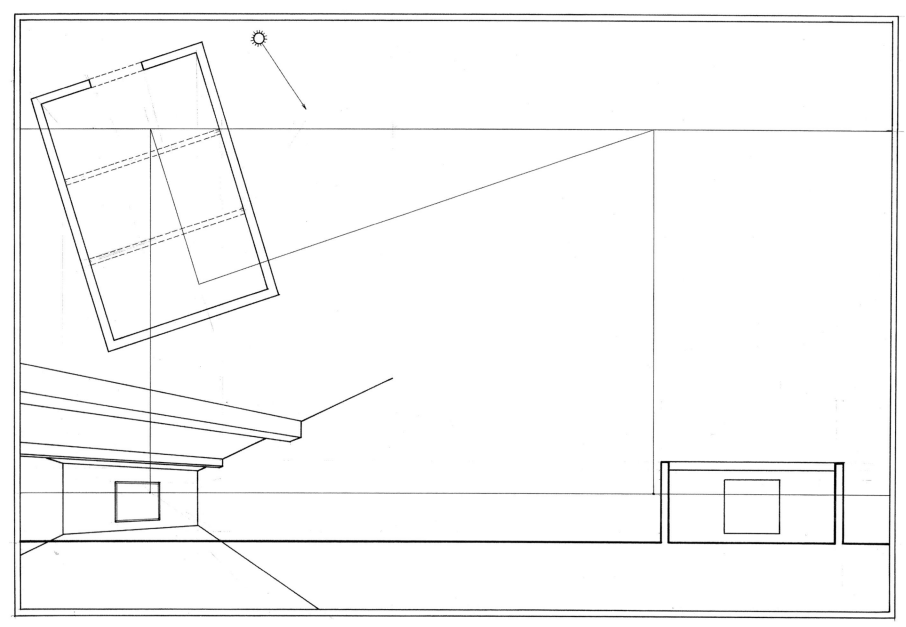

D.7 Shade and shadow in perspective projection, Exercise 2.

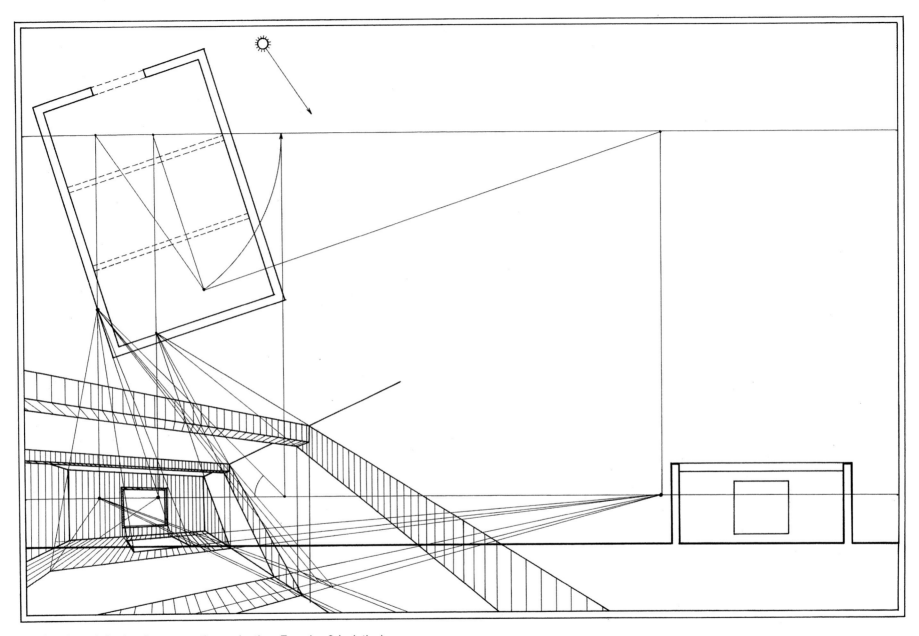

D.8 Shade and shadow in perspective projection, Exercise 2 (solution).

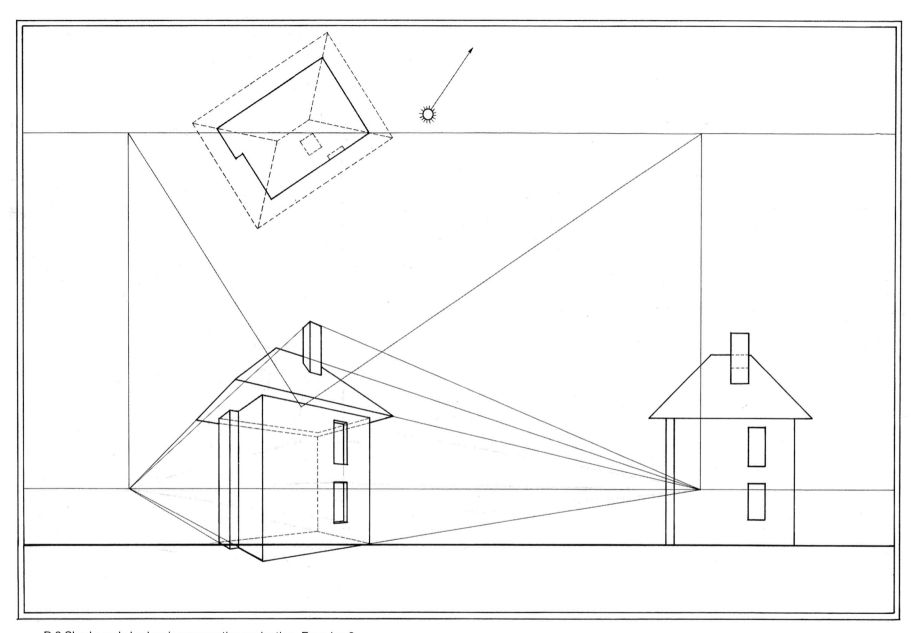

D.9 Shade and shadow in perspective projection, Exercise 3.

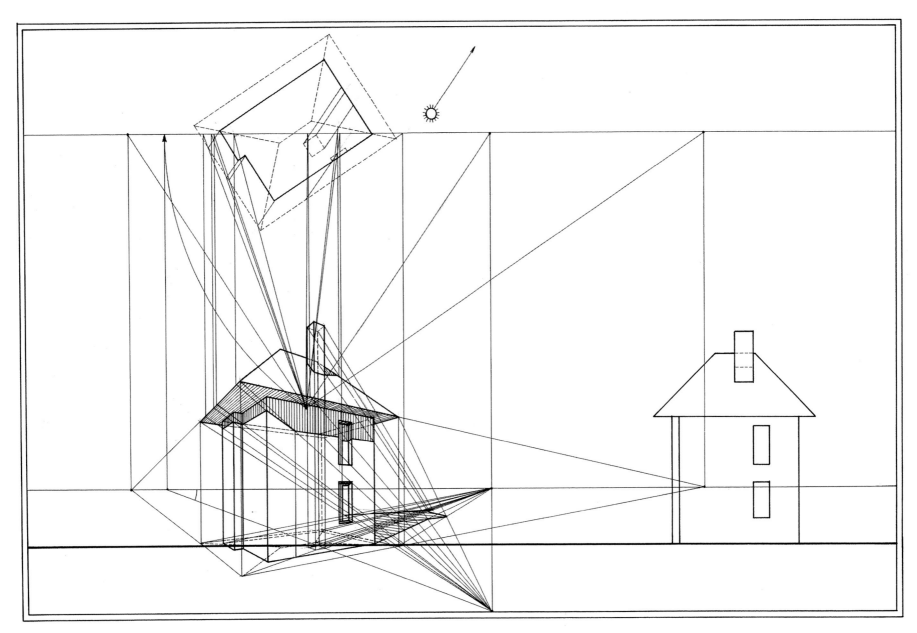

D.10 Shade and shadow in perspective projection, Exercise 3 (solution).

Bibliography

Allport, Floyd H. *Theories of Perception and the Concept of Structure.* New York: John Wiley & Sons, Inc., 1955. Provides an overview of the process of perceiving as well as in-depth discussion on of various points of view including gestalt psychology and transactional psychology.

Arnheim, R. *Art and Visual Perception.* new version. Berkley and Los Angeles: University of California Press, 1974. Arnheim's central work considers the perception and representation of shape, form, and space from the perspective of gestalt psychology. Includes analysis of the development of drawings by children.

Arnheim, R. *Visual Thinking.* Berkley and Los Angeles: University of California Press, 1969. More wide- ranging in its scope than *Art and Visual Perception.* Considers visual perception as a cognitive activity that is both separate from and related to other modes of thought.

Arnheim, R. "Gestalt Psychology and Artistic Form" in *Aspects of Form.* Edited by L.L. Whyte. Bloomington: Indiana University Press, 1966, pp. 196–208.

Barnett, H. G. *Innovation: the Basis of Cultural Change.* New York: McGraw Hill, 1953. Account of the dynamics of perception during the process of design from the general perspective of gestalt psychology. Appendix, "On Things," provides an excellent account of the perception of qualities of things.

Blanshard, Francis Bradshaw. *Retreat from Likeness in the Theory of Painting.* New York: Columbia University Press, 1949. Provides a brief account from several points of view of the role of appearance in making pictorial art. Includes summaries of the positions of Plato, Aristotle, Reynolds, Plotinus, and Shopenhauer.

Boring, E. G. *Sensation and Perception in the History of Experimental Psychology.* New York: Appleton, 1942. Provides an historical account of changing understandings of perception and changing interpretations of specific phenomena including the primary and secondary depth cues.

Cooper, D. "Drawings as Substitute Places" in *Dichotomy.* Edited by G. Dodds. Detroit: University of Detroit School of Architecture, 1983, pp. 76–83.

Deregowski,J. B. "Pictorial Perception and Culture" in *Readings from Scientific American.* Edited by R. Held. San Francisco: W. H. Freeman Co., 1971, pp 79-85. Based on studies of Zulu tribesmen, presents evidence that visual perception and specifically linear perspective are culturally based.

Dewey, John. *Art as Experience.* A view of art presented by one of the central figures within the transactionalist point of view.

Edgarton, S. Y. *The Renaissance Rediscovery of Linear Perspective.* New York: Basic Books, 1975. Provocative and wide-ranging book that relates the rediscovery of linear perspective at the onset of the 1400s to developments in other fields including the arrival in Florence of a copy of Ptolemy's World Atlas, Columbus's voyage to America, and an overall changing world view. Book includes a detailed account of Brunelleschi's perspective experiments conducted in front of the Baptistery in Florence.

Edwards, Betty. *Drawing on the Right Side of the Brain.* New York: St. Martins Press, 1979. Presents a drawing pedagogy based on the model put forth by R. W. Sperry which proposed that spatial reasoning is a function of the right hemisphere of the brain and that verbal reasoning is a function of the left.

Gardner, Howard. *Art Mind and Body.* New York: Basic Books, Inc., 1982. By one of the central figures in Harvard's *Project Zero,* focuses on the artistic development of young children. Includes discussion of the noted child prodigy, Nadia and, as part of a general discussion of her case, takes a critical view of positions that have explained her case on the basis of a right-brain left brain split of functions. Discussion of children's art is preceded by a lengthy presentation of of several points of view on the correctness of a developmental model, among them, Jean Piaget, Naom Chomsky, Claude Lévi-Strauss, and Ernst Cassirer.

Gibson, J. J. *The Perception of the Visual World.* Boston: Houghton Mifflin, 1950. Gibson's first major work and the foundation for much of the second chapter of this volume. Though he would modify and expand his position in his later work (this work concentrates on the retinal image), this book lays the groundwork for Gibson's radical view that the environment provides sensory data that is in itself already ordered.

Gibson, J. J. *The Senses Considered as Perceptual Systems.* Boston: Houghton Mifflin, 1966. Provides significant modification and breadth to his earlier work, *The Perception of the Visual World.* Here he gives greater emphasis to the role of both kinesthetic interaction with the environment and the interaction of the senses with each other.

Gibson, J. J. *The Ecological Approach to V isual Perception.* Boston: Houghton Mifflin, 1979. Gibson's concluding work in which he returns to his original focus on visual perception. Study of the role of movement as a constant condition of the observer is used to posit the ambient optical array as a sufficient condition for vision.

Gombrich, E. H. *Art and Illusion* . Princeton NJ: Princeton University Press, 1960. Gombrich's powerful study that considers pictorial representation from the multiple perspectives current in modern psychology. Gombrich draws significantly from gestalt psychology, and transactional empiricism, as well as from the formative work of J. J. Gibson.

Gombrich, E. H. *The Image and the Eye* . Ithaca: Cornell University Press, 1982. Gombrich continues the direction of his earlier work, *Art and Illusion,* but in this volume builds more significantly on the mature work of J. J. Gibson.

Gombrich, E. H. "Meditations on a Hobby Horse" in *Aspects of Form,* Edited by L.L. Whyte. Bloomington: Indiana University Press, 1966, pp. 209–228. Gombrich's oft-cited parable on the mechanisms of representation. This work is key to the formulation of drawing as an act of making that is presented in the third chapter of this volume.

Gregory, R. L. *Eye and Brain.* 3d ed. New York: McGraw Hill, 1978. Readable volume introducing the broad issues of visual perception. Includes discussion of the physiology of seeing and explanations from various points of view of noted visual illusions and linear perspective.

Haldane, J. B. S. "On Being the Right Size," in *World of Mathematics.* New York: Simon and Schuster, 1956, Vol. 2, pp 952–957.

Harwood, A. C. *The Recovery of Man in Childhood.* Spring Valley, NY: Anthroposophic Press, 1958. Provides an excellent summary of the relationship of Steiner's pedagogy to Goethe and a year by year overview of the Waldorf School curriculum.

Ittleson, W. *The Ames Demonstrations in Perception.* Princeton: Princeton University Press, 1952. Documents the noted demonstrations conducted by Adelbert Ames Jr. that have provided significant support for the transactional position.

Koffka, Kurt. *Principles of Gestalt Psychology.* New York: Harcourt Brace & Co., 1935.

Köhler, Wolfgang. *Gestalt Psychology.* New York: H. Liveright, 1929.

Lorenz, Konrad. "The Role of Gestalt Perception in Animal and Human Behavior" in *Aspects of Form.* Edited by L.L. Whyte. Bloomington: Indiana University Press, 1966, pp. 157–178. Excellent account of the mechanism of perception as understood from the perspective of gestalt psychology.

McKim, Robert H. *Experiences in Visual Thinking.* Monterey: Brooks/Cole Co., 1972. Addresses representation and its relationship to creativity and design process.

Pirenne, M. H. *Optics, Painting and Photography.* Cambridge: Cambridge University Press, 1970. Optics of both the generation and viewing of perspective drawings. Limitations of perspective as a representation of the visual field are addressed. Includes a description of projective procedures used in executing the ceiling fresco at S. Ignazio by the Pozzo family.

Panofsky, Erwin. "Die Perspektive als Symbolische Form" in *Vorträge der Bibliothek, Warburg.1924-25* Berlin-Leipzig: 1925, pp.258–330.. Influential paper that presents a critique of perspective on optical and artistic grounds. As for the latter, it considers its limitations both from the well known position of Plato (ie. perspective distorts reality) and from his own position: perspective objectifies subjective reality. Panofsky also identifies a paradox of perspective particularly as it develops in Northern Europe; while, on the one hand, it closes pictures from a former religious role as a vehicle of religious symbolic order, it also opens a new role, within the Baroque, as a vehicle of religious vision.

Spock, Marjorie. *Teaching as a Lively Art.* Spring Valley, NY.: The Anthroposophic Press, 1978. Readable account of Rudolf Steiner education (including painting and drawing) from kindergarten through the eighth grade. Rich with personal accounts by the author.

Segal et al. *The Influence of Culture on Visual Perception.* New York: Bobbs Merril Co.,

1966. Looks at visual perception (and within that some well known visual illusions) from the stance of cultural relativism.

Warren, Richard M. and Roslyn P. *Helmholtz on Perception.* New York: John Wiley, 1968. Presents a brief history of the key nineteenth century empiricist and forerunner of present day transactional empiricism, Hermann L. F. Helmholtz. Includes original treatises of Helmholtz on questions of visual perception together with commentary by the authors on each.

White, John. *The Birth and Rebirth of Pictorial Space.* Boston: Boston Book and Art Shop,

1967. Addresses pictorial space at the critical juncture before and after Brunelleschi's perspective demonstration. Includes discussion of the work of Cimabue, Giotto, Masaccio, Donatello, Ghiberti, Paolo Uccello, and the Sienese masters. It concludes with a brief look back at the pictorial space of imperial Rome, in particular the frescoes of Pompeii.

Winner, Ellen. *Invented Worlds.* Camridge: Harvard University Press, 1982. Along with Howard Gardner one of the central figures in Harvard's *Project Zero.* Book provides a good overview of psychological issues as they relate to the arts. Particularly strong in its explanations of children's art.

Wright, L. *Perspective in Perspective.* London: Routledge & Kegan Paul, 1983. In depth account of the history and techniques of perspective from the Greeks and Romans to the present day. Provides detailed accounts of Alberti's method of generating perspectives with distance points, Piero della Francesca and Paolo Uccello's generation of perspectives from plans, and the Pozzo family's technique for projecting the ceiling fresco at S, Ignazio in Rome.

Glossary

Accommodation. Depth cue conditioned on the eye's changing focal length in viewing objects at various distances.

Aerial perspective. Depth cue conditioned on the effect of air on the color and visual acuity of objects at various distances from the observer.

Axonometric projection. System of projection including isometry and dimetry. Objects are positioned in an attitude tilted to the picture plane and projected to the picture plane with orthogonal (lines at 90°) sight lines. Axonometric views are drawn to scale, represent all three faces of a rectangular object (front, top, and side), and show parallel lines as parallel.

Bird's eye view. Steeply inclined downward looking perspective view. Bird's -eye views yield a strong sense of the plan of an object or scene.

Center of vision. In perspective drawing, the point at which the viewer is looking on the picture plane.

Chiaroscuro. From the Italian *chiaro*, meaning light and *oscuro*, meaning dark, a technique of drawing which represents a full range of value from light to dark typically on a gray background.

Cone of vision. In perspective drawing, a conical field of vision radiating out from the viewer's eyes. Equivalent to the term breadth of field as it would be understood by a photographer. Typical cones of vision used in perspective range from 30° to 60° and rarely exceed 90°.

Contour. Lines on the surfaces of objects generated by profiles, interior edges, and surface textures.

Convergence. 1. Depth cue conditioned on the angle at which the two eyes must converge in viewing an object in close proximity to the viewer. **2.** In perspective drawing, the phenomenon of parallel lines appearing to come together at common vanishing points.

Depth cues. Conditions in the visual field that yield a perception of depth. Depth cues are generally divided in two groups: primary cues which are conditioned on the existence of two eyes, and secondary cues which are independent of the existence of two eyes.

Dimetric projection. A type of axonometric projection in which two of an objects spatial axes describe equal angles relative to the picture plane.

Disparity vision. Depth cue conditioned on the disparity between the views from the two eyes in viewing objects that in close proximity to the viewer.

Ecological psychology. An understanding of perception that emphasizes the contribution of the order implicit in the environment The principal advocate of this position is James J. Gibson.

Elevation. A horizontally directed orthographic view of a vertical face of an object or space.

Empathy. Sharing the same emotions or sensations as another person. In this text

empathy is understood to be transferable to inanimate things.

Foreshortening. The apparent reduction in size of elements on longitudinal surfaces (surfaces that are turned relative to the viewer) with greater distance from the observer.

Gestalt psychology. An understanding of perception that emphasizes the role of predisposing laws in the process of perception.

Ground line. In perspective drawing, a line on the picture plane where the ground plane or assumed ground plane meets the picture plane

Horizon line. In perspective projection, a line on the picture plane which is level to the ground, passes through the center of vision, and represents the height of the viewer's eyes.

Isometric Projection. From the Greek *iso*, meaning same, and *metron*, meaning measure. A type of axonometric projection in which all three of an objects spatial axes describe equal angles relative to the picture plane.

Magic method A method for constructing one-point perspectives using elevations or sectional views.

Motion parallax. Depth cue conditioned on differences between apparent optical motions of objects at various distances from an observer who is moving.

One-point perspective. The characteristic perspective view resulting from viewing in a direction that is parallel to the major spatial axis of an object or space.

Orthographic projection. System of projection including, plans, elevations, and sections. Objects are positioned in an attitude parallel to the picture plane and projected to the picture plane with orthogonal (lines at 90°) sight lines. Orthographic views are drawn to scale, show parallel lines as parallel, represent frontal surfaces without distortion of shape or proportion, and represent only one face of a rectangular object.(front, top, or side).

Overlap. Depth cue conditioned on near objects overlapping distant objects.

Oblique projection. System of projection including, plan oblique and elevation oblique views. Objects are positioned in an attitude parallel to the picture plane and projected to the picture plane with *oblique* (lines at angles other than 90°) sight lines. Oblique views are drawn to scale, show parallel lines as parallel, represent frontal surfaces without distortion of shape or proportion, and represent all three faces of a rectangular object.(front, top, and side). See also Paraline views

Paraline views. Not a system of projection itself but rather a category of projective systems. Includes those systems such as axonometric and oblique projection that show tall three faces of objects and at the same time maintain parallel lines as parallel.

Perspective, linear. 1. Depth cue conditioned on the apparent convergence of parallel lines with greater distance from the observer.

2. Drawing system built on the convergent projection of parallel lines to common vanishing points and on the convergent projection of sight lines to a single station point, the position of the viewer.

Pictorial depth cues. Those depth cues that are independent of the existence of two eyes and can be represented on a two dimensional plane.

Picture plane. A plane, analogous to a window, through which drawings are projected.

Plans. A vertically directed orthographic view of a top or bottom face of an object or space.

Sections. A horizontally directed orthographic view into the inside of an object or space.

Shade and shadow. Depth cue predicated on the information provided by shade and shadow.

Sight line. A line used to project points on an object to equivalent positions on a picture plane. Sight lines can vary in their attitude to the picture plane; in orthographic and axonometric projection, they are always orthogonals (at 90°); in oblique projection they are oblique (at angles other than 90°); in perspective projection they converge at a single point, the station point, the position of the viewer.

Size perspective. Depth cue conditioned on the apparent reduction in size of objects (of known size) with greater distance from the observer.

Spatial armature. A geometric framework of coordinates on which a drawing can be constructed.

Station point. In perspective projection, the point representing the position of the viewer to which convergent sight lines are drawn

Surface texture. Term used by James J. Gibson to mean any condition of surface that reflects light that varies from light to dark across its surface.

Textural gradient. Term used by James J. Gibson to mean the condition at the point of impact of light on the retina that corresponds in an ordinal manner (point for point) to the texture from which light has been reflected.

Transactional psychology or transactional empiricism. An understanding of perception that emphasizes the contributions of learning and interaction with the environment to the process of perceiving. Principal advocates of this position are John Dewey and Adelbert Ames.

Two-point perspective. The characteristic perspective view resulting from viewing in a direction that is diagonal to both major spatial axis of an object or space.

Upward position in visual field. Depth cue predicated on the tendency of objects to be seen against the background of a continuous ground or floor surface. Objects that are farther tend to be located higher in the visual field and those that are nearer tend to be located lower in the visual field.

Vertical measuring line. In perspective drawing, a line on the picture plane used to generate vertical information at scale.

Vanishing point. In perspective projection, a point on the picture plane at which a set of parallel lines appears to converge.

Visual field. The sensation of vision projected on the retina. ie. sensation as against perception.

Index

NOTES

NOTES

NOTES

NOTES

NOTES

NOTES

NOTES

NOTES

ABOUT THE CD-ROM

Introduction

This appendix provides you with information on the contents of the CD that accompanies this book. For the latest and greatest information, please refer to the ReadMe file located at the root of the CD.

System Requirements

- A computer with a processor running at 120 Mhz or faster
- At least 32 MB of total RAM installed on your computer; for best performance, we recommend at least 64 MB
- A CD-ROM drive

Using the CD with Windows

To install the items from the CD to your hard drive, follow these steps:

1. Insert the CD into your computer's CD-ROM drive.
2. The CD-ROM interface will appear. The interface provides a simple point-and-click way to explore the contents of the CD.

If the opening screen of the CD-ROM does not appear automatically, follow these steps to access the CD:

1. Click the Start button on the left end of the taskbar and then choose Run from the menu that pops up.
2. In the dialog box that appears, type **d:\start.exe.** (If your CD-ROM drive is not drive d, fill in the appropriate letter in place of d.) This brings up the CD Interface described in the preceding set of steps.

What's on the CD

Videos of the author teaching selected exercises from the text. Where appropriate, a still photo of the subject being drawn is included for self-practice. Before you begin the exercises, please be sure to watch the introduction video included on the CD. Some important points are discussed in this video, including how the book contents relate to the video exercises and how to best use these video exercises and any corresponding still images.

PLEASE NOTE:
You must have QuickTime 7.0 (or later) to view the movie files on this CD-ROM

To download or upgrade please visit:
http://www.apple.com/quicktime/download/win.html

For questions about downloading QuickTime or viewing the movie files using QuickTime please visit:
http://www.apple.com/support/quicktime/

If you have trouble viewing the still images (.jpg format) you can try adjusting your default picture viewer by following these instructions:
http://support.microsoft.com/kb/307859

If you still cannot view the images please visit Wiley's Tech Support website:
http://www.wiley.com/techsupport

Customer Care

If you have trouble with the CD-ROM, please call the Wiley Product Technical Support phone number at (800) 762-2974. Outside the United States, call 1(317) 572-3994. You can also contact Wiley Product Technical Support at http://support.wiley.com. John Wiley & Sons will provide technical support only for installation and other general quality control items. For technical support on the applications themselves, consult the program's vendor or author.

To place additional orders or to request information about other Wiley products, please call (877) 762-2974.

CUSTOMER NOTE: IF THIS BOOK IS ACCOMPANIED BY SOFTWARE, PLEASE READ THE FOLLOWING BEFORE OPENING THE PACKAGE.

This software contains files to help you utilize the models described in the accompanying book. By opening the package, you are agreeing to be bound by the following agreement:

This software product is protected by copyright and all rights are reserved by the author, John Wiley & Sons, Inc., or their licensors. You are licensed to use this software on a single computer. Copying the software to another medium or format for use on a single computer does not violate the U.S. Copyright Law. Copying the software for any other purpose is a violation of the U.S. Copyright Law.

This software product is sold as is without warranty of any kind, either express or implied, including but not limited to the implied warranty of merchantability and fitness for a particular purpose. Neither Wiley nor its dealers or distributors assumes any liability for any alleged or actual damages arising from the use of or the inability to use this software. (Some states do not allow the exclusion of implied warranties, so the exclusion may not apply to you.)